ARE WE LIVING IN THE

LAST DAYS?

ARE WE LIVING IN THE
LAST DAYS?

FOUR VIEWS OF THE HOPE WE SHARE
ABOUT REVELATION AND CHRIST'S RETURN

BRYAN CHAPELL

BakerBooks

a division of Baker Publishing Group
Grand Rapids, Michigan

© 2024 by Bryan Chapell

Published by Baker Books
a division of Baker Publishing Group
Grand Rapids, Michigan
BakerBooks.com

Printed in the United States of America

Library of Congress Cataloging-in-Publication Data
Names: Chapell, Bryan, author.
Title: Are we living in the last days? : four views of the hope we share about revelation and Christ's return / Bryan Chapell.
Description: Grand Rapids, Michigan : Baker Books, a division of Baker Publishing Group, [2024] | Includes bibliographical references.
Identifiers: LCCN 2023014293 | ISBN 9781540903921 (paper) | ISBN 9781540903938 (casebound) | ISBN 9781493444700 (ebook)
Subjects: LCSH: End of the world. | Eschatology.
Classification: LCC BT877 .C46 2024 | DDC 236/.9—dc23/eng/20230710
LC record available at https://lccn.loc.gov/2023014293

Italics added to direct Bible quotations reflect the author's emphasis.

Baker Publishing Group publications use paper produced from sustainable forestry practices and post-consumer waste whenever possible.

24   25   26   27   28   29   30   7   6   5   4   3   2   1

To Kathy

By the wondrous blessing of God
an heir together with me of the grace of life and eternity.

Contents

Contents

Introduction

T hough it happened several years ago, I could take you to the precise location where a dear woman, who loved me and wanted to protect me, whispered a warning. As I passed her pew to greet early arrivers for the worship service, she caught my arm and pulled me down close enough that no one else could hear her say, "My friends say you don't believe that Jesus is coming back."

Don't You Believe Jesus Is Coming Back?

In waves, I was first shocked, then angry, then sad. Of course I believe that Jesus is coming back. He said to his disciples, "I will come again and will take you to myself" (John 14:3). That's all the proof I need. I have preached this for over forty years. I look forward to Jesus's return. I believe he is coming again. I pray for that day. Why would anyone say or suspect anything different?

A generation earlier, our historic church had been pastored for many years by a highly effective and faithful man who held a different view from mine of how the last days before Christ's return will unfold. I had been honest about these differences when the church invited me to be its pastor, and I encouraged the congregation not to make too much of them since we were together on all the essentials of the gospel. I said, "Let me pastor and preach for a couple of years so that you trust I'm committed to Christ and Scripture. Then we'll be ready to study together what the Bible says about the end times."

The two years passed, and with the encouragement of our church's leaders I boldly launched into a sermon series on Daniel, one of the Bible's most prophecy-filled books. Still, I have a few grains of pastoral discretion in my noggin. Even though that influential pastor had gone to be with the Lord more than twenty years before my arrival, I thought it would be best to precede the sermon series with a multi-evening seminar on some of the different views of the end times that have been held by Bible-believing leaders around the globe and through the centuries.

I tried to be fair in presenting the viewpoints of those with whom I differed. I attempted to show the biblical arguments each historic view uses to support its distinctions. Finally, I affirmed the faith of all who held to the essentials of salvation by grace through faith in the shed blood and bodily resurrection of God's Son. "Good people may differ on some of these end-times matters," I generously offered. Then I concluded, "But we all agree that Jesus died for our sins, rose in victory over them, and is coming back to judge the wicked and welcome his people to heaven's eternal blessings."

I'm sure that in my heart I congratulated myself for such a good, thorough, fair, and biblical presentation. Later, I was able to go through the Daniel sermon series with much appreciation from the people who shook my hand as they left church each Sunday. I thought, *We've tackled the end-times controversies and come through unscathed.*

Then this dear lady tells me that the consequence of all my pastoral preparation, preaching, and prayer is that her friends in the church think that I don't believe Jesus is coming back.

Dominoes, Details, and Differences

I was experiencing what many other pastors have feared and fought: people can get so attached to a particular view of end-times prophecies that if you don't agree with them, then they think you don't believe the Bible. They further reason, "Since you don't believe the Bible, then you might not believe Jesus is coming back at all. You might not even be a Christian."

The consequence of these thought dominoes is that some people become even more devoted to the details of a particular view of the end times (also called the last days). They seem determined to figure out where we are on the biblical timeline of the coming of the antichrist, the length of the tribulation, and the identity of the assembling nations that battle at Armageddon. However, most people shy away from such controversies and details. Believing that the matters are more complex than ordinary Christians can calibrate, they cling to a basic belief that Jesus is coming back but leave the prophetic particulars to the more informed preachers and internet junkies who love illustrated timelines and study insights into how our nightly news connects to biblical prophecies.

Most Christians don't remember the exact sequence of the rapture, the antichrist, the tribulation, and Armageddon. They only have a general sense that Christ is supposed to come from heaven to take us back to heaven. That basic perception is occasionally spiced with popular movie or bestselling book images of raptured pilots disappearing from planes in midflight, an antichrist who appears to be either the devil or the latest president we don't like, tank columns on the fields of Israel with jets or UFOs flying above, and a lake of fire before a judgment throne that looks strangely like what Dorothy and her friends faced in *The Wizard of Oz.*

Christians who are more serious about biblical prophecy may have their financial stewardship and political preferences largely affected by ministries that emphasize God's special plans for the nation of Israel, the necessity of God's Word being available to the whole world prior to Christ's return, or warnings about things such as a common currency, European alliances, universal vaccinations, or anything that contains the number 666. Few of these people are aware that these perspectives are not shared among all serious Christians but result from views of biblical prophecy whose foundations predetermine our conclusions. If you start with a different foundation, you will get a different conclusion.

For example, certain views of the end times only work if you presume that the Jewish prophets of the Old Testament did not foresee the church age that we live in now—an age in which most believers are not ethnic Jews. Other views are based on the assumption that God wants to reestablish the laws of Israel for the whole world. Some views presume that the world will only continue to get worse, but others think the gospel will make the world get better over time. Some believe that Jesus will reign upon the earth for a thousand years prior to his final return and judgment. Others think that we may be thousands of years from Christ's return. Still others think we're already living in Christ's thousand-year reign and only those who believe Jesus's return and judgment could happen at any time are being faithful to him.

The Main Reason for Biblical Prophecy

These differing perspectives affect how some Christians want their political leaders to allocate billions of dollars in foreign aid or military resources, as well as how they want mission organizations to prioritize their efforts. Yet political, military, and mission policies are not the only, or even the main, reason the Bible includes marvelous revelations of the events that precede and characterize Christ's return. The main reason Scripture gives us prophetic views of our future path to heaven is to provide the encouragement we need to endure faithfully our present days on earth with confidence in God's eternal promises (Rom. 15:4).

We need to know that the evil, pain, and trials we now face are not God's last word or our final destiny. As we manage seemingly endless days of disappointment, grief, or failure, we may never see enough of this world's consolations to make sense of God's plans or to remain faithful to his purposes. So our loving God pulls back the curtain to our future through biblical prophecies that not only reveal his final destination for us but also provide key markers to give us hope along the way. Without the assurance these markers provide, we would weary of our journey toward heaven and possibly doubt that God could sustain us and his purposes through the many twists, trials, and tragedies.

Without God's promises of eternity and revelations of what happens before we get there, we couldn't remain faithful on earth. So God reveals his loving heart and sovereign hand in biblical prophecies to strengthen our hearts for both everyday living and extraordinary trials. Ultimately, the Bible's prophecies are meant to dry our tears, fuel our endurance, and brighten our paths so that we can fulfill God's purposes with confidence in his promises. Every prophecy is meant to provide us strength for today and hope for tomorrow.

The Map of Assurance

Of course, not every prophecy is equally clear, but that doesn't diminish its value or our need for the biblical heads-up. Many prophecies function as landmarks on a map to our future. How do we view and use such landmarks?

Take the example of when a friend gives us a map to a holiday spot. They may mark it with a note saying, "You'll pass a fruit stand just before you make the last turn." As we are traveling, we may begin to wonder exactly what the fruit stand will be like. Will it be large or small? Will it sell apples, watermelons, peaches, or mangos? People in our car may have different ideas of what a fruit stand in that region sells, whether it will be indoor or outdoor, and how near it sits to the road.

Yet, despite all the questions and speculations, when our journey takes us by the fruit stand, we will say, "Aha, that's it!" The map doesn't give every dimension and detail of each landmark because then it would be too complex and maybe too intimidating to be of help. But what we need to know to find our way, to have the encouragement to keep going, and to have the assurance we need to keep following the map becomes clear as its landmarks come into view. We don't necessarily know every feature before we arrive at the landmarks, but each has sufficient description for us to recognize it as it comes into view so that we will have the assurance we need to keep following the map.

United by Scripture and Mission

A few years ago, this assurance that all Christians need to march into the future with confidence that they're on God's path led the leaders of the wonderful organization Bible Study Fellowship (BSF) to prepare a survey of the book of Revelation for study groups around the world. During all the years that BSF leaders had led tens of thousands of new and mature believers through in-depth Bible study, they hadn't covered the book of Revelation as an international study. They thought its prophetic material would be too controversial. However, the questions BSF participants kept asking ultimately led the organization's leaders to believe that they were depriving members of needed biblical truth.

BSF decided it was necessary to teach Revelation for members to grasp the fullness of God's faithfulness. Still, BSF leaders had to face the likelihood of controversy. To model how to deal with differences and still unite around the Bible's essentials, BSF invited teachers with differing perspectives on Revelation to conduct its international training. The first was Mark Bailey, former president of Dallas Theological Seminary and a longtime friend of mine. When I was the president of the Fellowship of Evangelical Seminary Presidents, Mark was its vice president. The second person was Walt Kaiser, another dear friend who was a long-term president of Gordon-Conwell Theological Seminary and previously had been the dean at Trinity Evangelical Divinity School. BSF also invited me.

What I was asked to explain at that meeting has become the basis for this book. First, I gave a little bit of the history behind the perspectives represented by these faithful men who were leading the meeting with me. When the generations preceding ours were establishing the foundations of Bible-believing evangelicalism in this nation, the Bible was under attack. Many godly men and women sacrificed their careers and financial futures to oppose liberal theology in the dominant churches of their day and to establish institutions and churches that would uphold the truth of Scripture.

These Bible-believing leaders worked together across denominational and dispensational divides, knowing that the cause of Christ and the defense of Scripture needed to supersede our differences on end-times perspectives. But once evangelical churches and institutions were established, it became much easier for our differences about the end times to divide and even embitter our branches of Bible-believing Christianity.

Entire churches, denominations, and movements became like the dear women in my church whom I described at the beginning of this chapter. They so closely identified one perspective on end-times prophecies as being "what the Bible teaches" that they doubted any *real* Christian would believe anything different. Thankfully, the Lord gave me enough time to preach his Word and love his people that any doubts about my belief in Christ's return were ultimately erased. The years of ministry in that church became one of God's greatest blessings to me and my family. Similar blessings flowed upon the BSF gathering when those of us who were leading and differed about some aspects of the end times still embraced one another as brothers in Christ.

My prayer, and the purpose of this book, is for similar blessings to flow across the Bible-believing churches of the United States and many other nations. The mission of Jesus Christ must take priority over decades-long antipathies that are driven by arguments about the last days based on details and origins that are foggy for most Christians. In fact, many younger Christians look at how end-times debates have divided previous generations of believers and determine to avoid controversy by steering away from any end-times teaching in the Bible. This is not only sad but also dangerous, because the passages of Scripture describing the last days were given by the Holy Spirit as necessary preparation for the faith challenges the world will throw at every generation.

Uniting in the essentials of biblical faith shouldn't require Christians to throw away their views of the end times, but we must find ways to work together for the cause of Christ in this present darkness. The cause of Christ requires us to recognize that in our lifetime we are facing some of the greatest challenges to biblical faith as well as the greatest numerical expansion of Christianity in the history of the world. The multiplication of followers of Jesus in Asia, Africa, and the Muslim world is astounding. Working together to face our challenges, to steward tremendous blessings, and to address these opportunities from the Holy Spirit is the present calling of all believers.

How can we differ on views of the last days and still unite in Christ's mission? What follows is the approach that was blessed at the international BSF gathering. After I recounted the history that unified me and my friends in the essentials of biblical faith, we were each given the opportunity to represent fairly our views and our differences about the end times. Then we all three affirmed that our differences on the end times should not separate us from being brothers in Christ. We are of one heart on the basics of the gospel, *and* we are of one mind on the most important details of the last days.

Despite our important differences, we agreed that we share the hope that Jesus will return to claim his loved ones, judge evil, and establish his eternal kingdom in which all believers of every age will experience his righteousness, restoration, and reunion. We all agree the Bible teaches these things and that those who believe them are genuine believers. This book follows a similar path because there really are wonderful truths about the end times that we can all affirm.

We need this unity because everyone needs to be strengthened by the hope of heaven for the challenges of earth. We need all that Scripture teaches to prepare for all that life will bring. We don't need to let—indeed, we should not let—some uncertainties and differences make us shy away from the most important truths the Bible teaches about the last days, because the Holy Spirit provided these truths to fuel the courage and stamina we need to honor Christ today. As we are honest and fair in representing different perspectives about the last days, as well as accurate about the hope that all Christians share, the Holy Spirit will unite our hearts for the work of the gospel today.

Prophecy for Simple People Like Me

I need to add a word here about how I plan to help *everyone* claim the hope we share. If you are a Bible prophecy expert, then this book is probably not for you. My intention isn't to go into refined Greek word studies or detailed speculations about the clothing of the antichrist, the weapons at Armageddon, the length of the lion's wings in Daniel 7, or the president who will be in office when Jesus returns. At the risk of acknowledging that this book may be characterized by some as "End Times for Dummies," my intention is simply to explain key features of the major views that Bible-believing people hold about future prophecies. As I do so, the most sophisticated scholars who read this book will discover that I don't relate all the details of all their views.

The way that I boil down each view to its basics to make it accessible isn't intended to disrespect the preachers and scholars who have expended so much of mind and heart to discern the wonders of God's plans. The church needs such biblical experts to guide us toward the future and to help us interpret our times. Still, I recognize that my explanations, illustrations, and timelines may not reflect all the nuances of the experts' thoughts, and they may grow frustrated with how I simplify matters to keep them clear in my own mind.

Others who may grow frustrated with me are those who hold so strongly to one end-times perspective that they aren't able to affirm the intellect or perhaps even the faith of those who disagree with them. I will only present end-times perspectives in this book that I believe are held by sincere, true believers in Jesus Christ. I won't question the faith of any. I may not do the best job of representing every variation of every view (and there are many), but I hope that Bible-believing Christians will finish this book with a basic understanding of both the differences and the commonalities between major perspectives on the last days that lead to our eternal destiny.

The Hope We All Share

My goal isn't that readers would simply *know* the different views but that as much as possible they would *share* a common hope: Jesus is coming back! He will return from heaven to gather to himself all those who have placed their faith in him. Those who have believed in him will live forever in perfect spiritual union with him and all who love him, with perfected bodies, in a perfect world. Those who don't love Christ Jesus will be judged by getting what they ultimately want: eternal separation from relationship with the God who created them. But no Christian will share that destiny.

So that we may be encouraged through present trials and prepared for our future home, God has given us information in his Word about the landmarks that we should anticipate on our journey to him. We may have different ways of interpreting those prophetic landmarks, but we can agree on the destination we share, and we should love and respect those who are on the journey to Jesus with us. The dear lady who warned me about those doubting my faithfulness shares my destiny. Those who doubted my faithfulness because I couldn't affirm the end-times view they had been taught also share my destiny. The long-faithful pastor who taught a view that differs from mine shares my destiny.

Because our destiny is the same, we share the hope of glory. All Christians do. I pray that this book will be accurate enough in its descriptions of our different end-times views that we will all be able to identify and be encouraged by the view we believe is most consistent with Scripture. I also pray this book will be clear enough in its descriptions of the common features of our views that we'll be able to praise God together for the hope we all share.

1

Are We Living
in the Last Days?

In 1988 a man named Edgar C. Whisenant wrote a booklet titled *88 Reasons Why the Rapture Will Be in 1988*. Over 300,000 copies were mailed to pastors free of charge, and 4.5 million copies were sold in bookstores and other outlets. When 1988 came and went without the rapture occurring, humorist Dave Barry had a field day. He wrote an article for the *Chicago Tribune* with the headline "Doomsayer Goofs—But, Hey, It's Not the End of the World." Here's part of what Barry said to his readers:

> In case you missed it, what happened last year was that a man named Edgar Whisenant, who is a former NASA rocket engineer, came out with a booklet in which he proved via exact mathematical calculations based on the Bible that the world was going to end in 1988, most likely on Sept. 12. . . . A lot of other True Believers around the country also got very excited over Mr. Whisenant's prediction, so you can imagine what a letdown it was when Sept.

12 rolled around and—as you know if you keep up with the news—the world did not end.[1]

Whisenant didn't give up. He decided that he had made a slight miscalculation in his math and was off by one year. So he wrote another booklet and titled it *The Final Shout: Rapture Report 1989*. That second disappointment led to three more booklets published in 1993, 1994, and 1997. But few people took Whisenant seriously because he had cried "Wolf!" too many times.

Unfortunately, failed predictions haven't stopped people throughout history from trying to calculate the timing of the last days to predict how near we are to Christ's return. One of the most famous examples was a man named William Miller (1782–1849). In 1818, after an intense two-year study of Scripture, especially in the book of Daniel, Miller wrote, "I was brought to the solemn conclusion that in about twenty-five years from that time [1818] all the affairs of our present state would be wound up."[2] To further confirm his astonishing discovery, Miller spent four more years in Bible study and became more convinced than ever that his findings were correct. Anthony Hoekema writes, "Miller did not at first set an exact date for Christ's return but affirmed that this event would occur 'about 1843.' Later, however, he specified that this return would take place sometime during the Jewish year running from March 21, 1843 to March 24, 1844."[3]

Miller was flooded with invitations to speak, which required constant travel. Finally, to keep up with demand, he wrote a sixty-four-page tract titled *Evidence from Scripture and History of the Second Coming of Christ, about the Year 1844*. He estimated that he had between 50,000 and 100,000 followers, but when the predicted year of the Lord's return passed without incident, his followers became disillusioned, and Miller himself confessed the following:

> Were I to live my life over again, with the same evidence that I then had, to be honest with God and man, I should have to do as I have

done. . . . I confess my error and acknowledge my disappointment; yet I still believe that the day of the Lord is near, even at the door; and I exhort you, my brethren, to be watchful, and not let that day come upon you unawares.[4]

In more recent times, *USA Today* reported on another failed attempt to predict the end of the world. This time the doomsayer was Harold Camping, an eighty-nine-year-old televangelist and former president of Family Radio. According to the article, one of the times Camping predicted the rapture would occur was on May 21, 2011. That was the day the world was supposed to end with a "series of worldwide earthquakes hitting at 6 p.m. People believed him. Some quit their jobs and nervously huddled in their homes awaiting their moment with God. The day of judgment didn't come. So, he pushed the date back to Oct. 21. Then, he stopped making predictions."[5] Camping died two years later at age ninety-two.

In Mark 13:32, Jesus actually warns his disciples about trying to predict the exact time of his return: "Concerning that day or that hour, no one knows, not even the angels in heaven, nor the Son, but only the Father." But his words haven't stopped countless people throughout history from trying to predict something that only the Father knows. Although Jesus's words alone should prevent people from making precise end-times predictions, there are additional reasons why such speculations are bound to lead to disappointment. I will offer a few of them in the following pages.

Interpreting the Book of Revelation

Almost anyone who wants to know about the events of the last days will eventually turn to the book of Revelation. Yet when we read Revelation, we immediately see that it's unlike any other New Testament book. Rather than focusing on the history and biography of Jesus and his followers or the doctrines and duties they taught, Revelation seems to take us into the realm of the imagination with fantastic beasts, thunderous voices, and vivid images. We encounter a dragon (12:3), a beast with seven heads and ten horns (13:1), another beast that speaks like a dragon but has two horns like a lamb (13:11), and a woman who sits on a seven-headed beast and has a mystery written on her forehead (17:3–5). A lamb gets married (19:7), dead people come to life (20:5), and a city drops down out of heaven to earth (21:2), and these are only selections from the wonders and horrors the book describes.

Also, unlike most of the material in the other New Testament books, the book of Revelation seems to point not to past history or present obligations but to things that are yet to occur (1:1–3). Among its prophecies, Revelation describes the coming of the four riders popularly known as the Four Horsemen of the Apocalypse (chap. 6), seven angels with seven plagues (chap. 15), and seven bowls of God's wrath (chap. 16). And, of course, the main character to ride onto the biblical stage in the book of Revelation is Jesus Christ himself, whose heavenly appearance is rich and wondrous in description:

> The hairs of his head were white, like white wool, like snow. His eyes were like a flame of fire, his feet were like burnished bronze, refined in a furnace, and his voice was like the roar of many waters. In his right hand he held seven stars, from his mouth came a sharp two-edged sword, and his face was like the sun shining in full strength. (Rev. 1:14–16)

> Then I saw heaven opened, and behold, a white horse! The one sitting on it is called Faithful and True, and in righteousness he judges and makes war. His eyes are like a flame of fire, and on his head are many diadems, and he has a name written that no one knows but himself. He is clothed in a robe dipped in blood, and the name by which he is called is The Word of God. (Rev. 19:11–13)

How can we make sense of all these images and descriptions? First, we need to understand that Revelation represents a specific type of writing in the Bible called "apocalyptic literature." *The Baker Illustrated Bible Dictionary* explains:

> The word "apocalypse" means "revelation." It is used in Rev. 1:1 to identify what follows as information that would otherwise only be known in heaven. "Apocalyptic" therefore refers to uncovering something that is hidden—revealing secrets. . . . As a literary form, apocalyptic literature might best be described as verbal cartoons. The images that are so graphically portrayed would have had, for the original readers, something of the instant impact that a political cartoon might have on us today. In order to understand such images, one must be familiar with the symbols being used.[6]

The use of the word *cartoon* may cause us to wince a bit—after all, this material is in God's Word—but we get the idea. Apocalyptic literature reveals things too great or mysterious for ordinary prose. So biblical writers explain these heavenly revelations in terms and images that stretch beyond the ways we ordinarily express experiences or expectations. They capture truths, times, and personalities using images, symbols, and signs that represent immense ideas, cataclysmic events, eons of time, spiritual wars, physical traumas, evil forces, and heavenly wonders. Some of these images and descriptions occur other places in Scripture, giving readers a context for interpreting their meaning. Other images and descriptions are tied to the culture, history, or language of the people who lived at the time this portion of the Bible was written.

The way we interpret apocalyptic literature, then, is either by comparing terms and images found elsewhere in Scripture or by researching history to determine how the original readers would have understood the author. Sounds simple enough, right?

Of course, it's not really simple at all or there wouldn't be so many debates about what Revelation means. All responsible interpreters consider comparison Scriptures and the author's cultural context, but different people make different comparisons and look at different contexts to figure out the meaning. That changes how they think Revelation should be interpreted.

Now, not everything is up for grabs. Don't give up on trying to understand. There are matters that everybody agrees on—that's what I pray this book will make clear over time. God has made crystal clear those matters that we need to know. The essential truths rise above question. Still, there are details that create controversies among us and probably won't be clarified until Christ's return. Our goal for the moment is to prepare for his coming as best we can in light of the prophetic landmarks that signal both the challenges we will face and the encouragements God has for us.

Remember that, no matter which perspective you prefer, the overall goal of the prophetic material is to encourage the enduring faithfulness of God's people amid the tears and trials of this present age (see Rev. 1:1, 3; 13:10; 14:12). So it's important to delve into this material even though we know there will be some divergence in explanations of the details. We don't have to know the exact timing of the events of the last days to benefit from knowing the types of events and experiences that lead up to Christ's return.

As godly interpreters consider Scriptural comparisons and historical contexts related to the book of Revelation, they have at least five ways of thinking about its events and experiences.[7]

1. *The Near View.* This view sees most of the prophecies in the book of Revelation as being fulfilled soon after they were written. The cataclysmic event near in both time and place to the writing of Revelation was the Roman destruction of the Jewish temple in AD 70. The events around the destruction of the temple created great persecutions and trials for both Jews and Christians as a cruel emperor and his army demolished Jerusalem and dispersed God's people.

Theologians refer to this near view of Revelation as *preterist*, which means "past." This view interprets key images and descriptions in Revelation as referencing matters future to its author but already past to us. So the book's prophetic details are thought to refer to specific people or events from the time of the apostles. For example, those with a near view may understand the mark of the beast (666) as a reference to the Roman emperor Nero, who persecuted Jews and Christians. In the language of Jesus's time, "Nero Caesar" could be represented numerically as 666, and some historians claim early Christians did this to speak secretly against the emperor.[8]

Near-view interpreters think Revelation was written to encourage first-century believers by showing how God planned to deliver them from the evil Roman Empire. This view isn't held by many evangelical Christians, but those who do hold it believe that everything necessary to prepare for Christ's return has already happened. That means according to this view we're already living in the last days.

2. *The Long View.* "This view asserts that the prophecies of the Apocalypse are an outline of church history and take place over a 2000+ years period of time, climaxing with Jesus' Second Coming."[9] Often those who hold this view think that the book of Revelation represents seven periods of church history: the opening chapters represent the birth and establishment of the early church; the breaking of the seals in chapters 4–7 symbolizes the fall of the Roman Empire; and the trumpet judgments in chapters 8–10 represent the invasions of the Roman Empire by the Vandals, Huns, Saracens, and Turks.

According to this interpretation, the later chapters of Revelation occur near to the time of the Protestant Reformation and focus on the antichrist, which many Reformation leaders believed was the pope. This Reformation perspective leads to the conclusion that chapters 11–13 represent the true church in its struggle against Roman Catholicism and the bowl judgments of chapters 14–16 represent God's judgment on the Catholic Church. All of these earlier periods are, then, understood to culminate in the future overthrow of Catholicism as depicted by the descriptions in chapters 17–19, followed by Christ's return in the final chapters to secure his and our eternal kingdom.[10]

Since this long view sees Revelation as largely describing the history of the church from Christ's time on earth until his final return to earth, theologians refer to it as *historicist*. Though long-view interpreters will vary as to which historical events are represented by Revelation's images and descriptions, they see much of Revelation's prophecy already fulfilled through God's unfolding plan for his church. This means, of course, that long-view Bible interpreters, despite their differences with near-view advocates, believe that we're living in the last days.

3. *The Future View*. This view sees most of the events and experiences of Revelation 4–22 as occurring in the future, so its adherents are called *futurists*. "Futurists divide the book of Revelation into three sections as indicated in 1:19: 'what you have seen, what is now and what will take place later.' Chapter 1 describes the past ('what you have seen'), chapters 2–3 describe the present ('what is now'), and the rest of the book describes future events ('what will take place later')."[11]

Probably most evangelical believers hold some version of this future view for the bulk of Revelation. Popular books in Christian bookstores, articles on the internet, and the occasional Christian movie typically reflect this view that seeks to help believers understand current events in the context of what must happen before or around Christ's future return. While most futurists don't try to predict the exact time of Christ's return, many look at recent world events—for example, the reestablishment of Israel as a home for the Jewish nation—as indications that Jesus will return in the near future.

Theologians with the most integrity don't try to say with certainty which world events correspond to most of Revelation's details, but they see much that has happened in the last century as possible fulfillments of biblical prophecy. Thus, it would be common for futurists to believe all that's necessary to precede Christ's return could have already occurred. Therefore, this view also places us in the last days.

4. *The Symbolic View.* This ancient view is built on the allegorical method of interpretation practiced by early church fathers such as Origen (AD 185–254) and Augustine (AD 354–420). They believed the Holy Spirit gave all of Scripture symbolic meaning beyond its apparent historical or biographical descriptions. Those who hold this view today claim that the book of Revelation doesn't so much refer to specific people or events but describes the ongoing spiritual battle between God and Satan. Since this perspective focuses on representing ideas about how good and evil interact prior to the triumph of Christ, theologians refer to it as *idealist.*

Those primarily holding to a symbolic understanding of Revelation believe that the apostle John's primary purposes for writing the book were to alert believers to ongoing spiritual struggles, equip them to engage those struggles, and encourage them to endure through the struggles with the promise that God will eventually triumph through Christ's return. Because this symbolic view doesn't require any specific historical event to occur prior to the second coming of Christ, idealists say that Jesus could come at any time. According to this perspective, the purpose of Revelation is preparation more than prediction, which would mean that we're already in the preparation period.

5. *The Mixed View.* While I have described the technical differences between the various views for interpreting Revelation, I expect that many people reading this book will see some validity in each of them. People who have been around different churches may sympathize—and maybe even agree—with two or three of these views. Few of us are experts on interpreting Revelation, and we tend to trust the spiritual leaders who have taught us over the years. If they have had different perspectives, our exposure to them has probably stirred the views together in our minds without our even being aware of the mix. So we become inclined to believe that elements from each of the views can inform our understanding of

Revelation. Our perspectives are influenced by our pastors, our background, our reading, and popular Christian culture.

Most of us have a mixed view. Not knowing all the technical differences and theological assumptions between the views, we become eclectic, taking a bit of prophetic perspective from people we trust, even if they don't agree with each other (and even if we don't know that). This isn't all bad. New Testament professor Scott Duvall explains that "this approach combines the strengths of several approaches, taking seriously the message to the original readers, acknowledging portions of the book that await future fulfillment, and finding relevant spiritual messages for Christians of every age."[12] If even the experts can be eclectic, then it's not a crime if we intentionally or unintentionally mix the views in our understanding.

Claiming Our Hope

This doesn't mean that we're just supposed to shrug our shoulders and say, "Oh well. Nobody knows for sure." That would cause us to dismiss the teaching of Revelation that the Holy Spirit inspired for our present encouragement and future endurance. I urged you earlier not to give up on trying to understand what the book of Revelation says about the end times. Now I hope you see the reason. What we have discovered in examining these different interpretive views is at least one consistent message: the last days are now!

Yes, interpretations vary about the timing, but we still pay attention to Revelation because it confirms what the Bible consistently teaches: we're already living in the last days. That means the book of Revelation and other biblical prophecies about the end times are immediately relevant to us. All the views we have examined agree on this. But how can this be, since some see the events and experiences of Revelation as future, some see them as past, and some see them as present? The answer is that all understand and agree that the end times of biblical history began before the book of Revelation was written.

We don't believe that we're living in the last days simply because different prophetic perspectives come to that same conclusion. Our reason for believing that we're already living in the end times is better than that—and much stronger. We believe that we're living in the end times because the Bible says so. The Holy Spirit revealed to the New Testament writers that they were already in the last days (Acts 2:16–17; Heb. 1:2; 1 John 2:18). Therefore, we who come after them are also in the last days before Christ's return.

What Are the End Times?

Before you are ready to agree that we're already living in the last days, you may need to consider how the Bible defines this time period. To do so, it's important not to depend on the fantastic images of a popular movie or the imaginative depictions of a bestselling author. They may offer great entertainment and can fire our imaginations (or give us nightmares) about our last days, but these depictions of the end times are usually too narrowly focused. To answer the questions "What are the end times?" and "When are the last days?" we need to distinguish between popular definitions and biblical definitions, since they're very different.

Those with a popular understanding of the end times are usually trying to identify which current events they can match up with Old and New Testament prophecies related to Christ's return. They think of the last days as a period immediately prior to Christ's return and marked by events predicted in biblical prophecies that are mostly still in the future for us. For example, the cover copy for one popular end-times book says, "Christians wonder whether the end times prophesied in the book of Revelation are upon us. Is the rising disorder we are experiencing a precursor of the approaching Rapture of the church and the final return of Christ?"[13]

Typically, such people look for key indicators of the end times in the news events of our day that seem consistent with prophetic descriptions in the Bible. For example, they may identify the rise to power of an enemy country or a controversial leader as the coming of an evil empire or the precursor to a one-world government or the first sign of the "beast" or the antichrist mentioned in Revelation. This popular approach to the end times keeps people vigilant for signs that indicate the last days will arrive soon or that we're already in them. But according to the biblical definition, we don't need to speculate whether we're living in the last days. They are here.

The Last Days Are Now

The end times began with the life, death, and resurrection of Jesus Christ and the pouring out of the Holy Spirit on the day of Pentecost. And the end times will continue until Jesus returns. Numerous New Testament passages show that we're living in the last days before Christ's second coming. Following are four specific examples.

Acts 2:14–21. On the day of Pentecost, the Lord poured out his Spirit on Jesus's disciples, and they began praising God in the languages of all the people who gathered around them. When some in the crowd wondered whether the disciples were drunk, Peter responded by saying, "These people are not drunk, as you suppose. It's only nine in the morning! No, this is what was spoken by the prophet Joel: 'In *the last days*, God says, I will pour out my Spirit on all people'" (vv. 15–17 NIV). Peter tells the crowd that they are seeing the fulfillment of Joel's prophecy about the last days.

Eckhard Schnabel, a professor of New Testament at Gordon-Conwell Theological Seminary, explains: "It should be noted that the phrase 'in the last days' in Acts 2:17 is an addition to the text of Joel, who begins this particular prophecy with the phrase 'and afterward.' Peter clarifies that what follows in Joel's prophecy relates to the last days of God's history of salvation: the end times as the new age that was ushered in by Jesus."[14]

We tend to calibrate the last days of biblical prophecy according to what we expect our own generation or near generations to experience. However, the Bible marks the end times by more expansive epochs. Prior to the fall of Adam and Eve, humanity lived in perfect harmony with the creation and the Creator. These were the first days of our walk with God. Then Adam's sin corrupted our world. We entered into "this present evil age" (Gal. 1:4). This age, however, can itself be divided into different eras: "these last days" since Christ came to earth for our salvation (Heb. 1:2), and the "former days" that preceded Jesus's first coming (Rom. 15:4).

When this present evil age began, we learned that we couldn't redeem ourselves from our sin or the corruption it caused. So our gracious God promised that he would send One who would save us from our sin and its consequences (Gen. 3:15). What followed were thousands of years of God's people anticipating the fulfillment of that promise. These millennia marked the age of God's promise of a coming Messiah. Throughout the days of that former period, God's people looked for their promised Redeemer. These former days—that were really thousands of years—of anticipation ended when Jesus came to earth.

When God sent Jesus to die for our sins, rise in victory over sin and death, and ascend to heaven to intercede for us, the time of anticipating our Savior concluded, but Jesus's work wasn't finished. He will yet come to judge the world, renew creation, and redeem his people. When those events occur, we'll enter the final epoch of our relationship with God that stretches into the blessings of eternity. In that time, God will establish the fullness of Christ's kingdom, and we'll forever be in perfect union with him and those who love him. But we are not there yet. Instead, we're living in another age of anticipation that marks the end times—the final era of our mortal existence, the last chapter of human history until the age of perfection that commences with Jesus's final return to earth.

The biblical writers, after so many millennia of anticipating Jesus's first coming, call the age in which we now live by various names, including "the last time/s" (Jude 1:18; 1 Pet. 1:20), "the last hour" (1 John 2:18), and "the end of the ages" (1 Cor. 10:11). They understood that Christ's first coming marked the conclusion of the age of promise and signaled this age of preparation for Christ's final return in glory.[15] No other epoch will have to pass. No other period will precede his coming. These are the last days that prepare for his return. So, these are the end times. The biblical writers encouraged their readers with this reality.

Hebrews 1:1–2. "Long ago, at many times and in many ways, God spoke to our fathers by the prophets, but *in these last days* he has spoken to us by his Son, whom he appointed heir of all things, through whom also he created the world." The author makes it clear that God's speaking through Jesus has happened "in these last days." In other words, the last days began with the ministry of Jesus and will continue until his final triumph.

James 5:1–9. In the first six verses of chapter 5, James indicts the rich people who abuse their workers and "have laid up treasure *in the last days*" (v. 3). He then assures his faithful readers that "the coming of the Lord is at hand" (v. 8) and their oppressors will not go unpunished because "the Judge is standing at the door" (v. 9). Clearly, James wants his readers to realize that because we live in the last days, that door could open at any moment.

First Peter 1:20–21. Peter tells his readers that Christ "was made manifest in the last times [also translated "at the end of the ages"] for the sake of you who through him are believers in God, who raised him from the dead and gave him glory." In his book *40 Questions about the End Times*, Dr. Schnabel tells us, "The phrase 'at the end of the ages' . . . reflects the early Christian conviction that the last period of history has been inaugurated" with the resurrection and ascension of Jesus.[16] We are in the final age that will culminate in Christ's final triumph.

The biblical view that we're living in the last period of ordinary human history is shared by most Bible-believing pastors and scholars, even though some focus more on the *conclusion* of the end times (the last of the last days) before Jesus returns. I emphasize this unity of perspective that we're in the last days to remind us all that Christ's coming is near. No other age or epoch will intervene. Yes, it's been two thousand years since Jesus promised to come again, but compared to the multiple millennia of hope that preceded his first coming, he is not delayed. Everything that needs to happen before Christ returns will happen in this age—our age. And since we cannot say with certainty how God will fulfill all that has been prophesied for the end times, Jesus could come at any moment.

Is that a new thought for you? I hope not.

His Appearing Is Imminent

The biblical teaching that we're already in the last days is sometimes called the "imminent appearing" of Jesus, and as we would expect, there are various perspectives on how much we should emphasize this understanding.[17] But there's no question that when God's people face trial or temptation, Scripture encourages us to remember that Jesus could come this week, this day, or this hour.[18] We should be prepared (Rev. 16:15).

Yes, there are different views on what must happen before Christ returns. Each view has different expectations and emphases.[19] Still, we should remind ourselves that his return will come like a thief in the night (2 Pet. 3:10). We won't know the day or the hour. The events that must occur prior to the second coming either have happened or could happen more quickly than anyone expects—a cascade of prophetic fulfillment, as when reports of the unraveling of the Soviet Union shocked the world in 1991. No national security expert in the West or the East expected so much power to unravel so quickly. Or consider how a totally unexpected COVID-19 pandemic changed our world's patterns, practices, and economies in only a few short months.

Another global pandemic, a multistate or multination drought, a hurricane undoing our power grid, an asteroid beyond telescope range, or a war in a distant nation interrupting supply chains for wheat, microchips, or rare earth elements could cripple the world and usher in prophetic realities far more quickly than any human could predict. And these are only the obvious calamities that could cascade into apocalyptic realities. We could add solar storms, supervolcanoes, genetic engineering mishaps, or artificial intelligence run amuck to the list of doomsday scenarios that could forever change life as we know it in seconds. On the other hand, perhaps fulfillment has already occurred in ways that we aren't prepared to recognize or among peoples we haven't properly regarded. The possibilities underscore the weight of Christ's words: "Concerning that day and hour no one knows" (Matt. 24:36).

What we know for sure is that these are the last days. So we live and give and pray and witness and work with the understanding that we must be responsible because we don't know the day or the hour. But we also must live and witness and sacrifice with awareness that this *could be* the final day and the final hour (1 Thess. 5:1–4). There's a tension between "it may be near" and "it may be far," but God intends to instill courage and compulsion for his purposes by the potential of Christ's return today (Matt. 24:6, 44).[20]

The tensions in the near and far interpretations form the basis for much of the next section of this book. I recognize that the explanations are about to become more complex and the debates a bit more intense. So before we go down that path, let's remind ourselves of the hope Bible-believing Christians share: the Savior who died for us is coming back for us—and he could come at any time.

Trying to anticipate the timing and details of his return so that we can prepare well has created some differences and disputes among God's people. Still, we must remember that those who share the hope of the return of a crucified and risen Savior will be gathered by him into his kingdom.

Therefore, as we cover views that describe the near and far perspectives on the prophecies that span the time from the first coming of Christ until his second coming, let's remember we are describing differences among those who are our eternal brothers and sisters in Christ.

The differences are important; the relationships are too.

2

Expectations for the End Times

Since we're living in the end times, we naturally wonder what the Bible says we should expect in this season of God's plan. We should remember that the end times began long before our lives and may continue long after, but that doesn't mean we have no clue for what will occur in this time frame.

The Bible clearly tells us many events and experiences that will occur in these last days. For example, in Matthew 24 Jesus tells his disciples that the following events will happen before he returns "on the clouds of heaven with power and great glory" (v. 30):

- Wars and rumors of wars (v. 6)
- Nation rising against nation (v. 7)
- Famines and earthquakes (v. 7)
- Tribulation, persecution, falling from faith, and betrayal (vv. 9–10)
- False prophets (v. 11)

- Increase of lawlessness (v. 12)
- Proclamation of the gospel to the whole world (v. 14)
- An abomination standing in the holy place (v. 15)
- False christs (v. 24)
- Sun and moon darkened with stars falling from heaven (v. 29)

Jesus included more details and predictions in this discourse, but the list I've extracted illustrates the tensions that can arise from the differing near and far interpretations of end-times prophecies.

Wars and Rumors of Wars

The last days most definitely include "wars and rumors of wars," but would those wars be *near* to the region of the Holy Land or *near* in time to the lives of Jesus's hearers? Jesus was speaking to his apostles when he said, "*You* will hear of wars and rumors of wars." So was he only talking about their immediate or local context? Or are the wars far away in time or place? Is Jesus speaking chronologically or geographically or both? Is the intended "you" who will "hear" of such wars the *near* apostles or *far* distant readers of Jesus's words such as you and me—or our children or generations yet to come?

If the wars were near to the place where Jesus made his predictions, then we still will have questions about which wars he references. Historians tell us that Jerusalem has been conquered almost fifty times since Jesus's day, with tens of thousands of Christians and Jews slaughtered in a number of those wars. So, if Jesus's words applied to the devastation of Jerusalem, which disaster did he predict? Aspects of the destruction of the temple by the Romans in AD 70 seem to align with many of Jesus's words. But the destruction of the Crusader army in 1187 that resulted in Muslim rule of the Holy City for centuries was also cataclysmic for God's people and could seem to fit other aspects of Jesus's prophecy (and the Christians of that era interpreted them that way). There were other wars that devastated Jerusalem in the past, and there may yet be wars that will devastate Jerusalem in the future.

If the prophesied wars relate to the Holy Land more generally, are they from the Roman period, the Crusader period, the Ottoman period, the world wars of the twentieth century, the modern Arab-Israeli conflicts, or the recent periods of surrounding conflicts in Iran, Iraq, Syria, and Afghanistan? If our interpretation isn't bound to the Holy Land, then the wars that precede the second coming could be on a global scale, such as those that once involved Mongols, Huns, and Turks; or more recently involved Germany, Italy, and Japan; or could yet involve Russia, China, European alliances, Arab alliances, and the United States. Such wars might include the devastation of conventional weapons, the utter destruction of atomic weapons, or the impact of technology yet to be discovered.

The Antichrist

The wars that Jesus references aren't the only sign of the end times that has an uncertain explanation. Jesus tells us that "false christs" will come before he comes (Matt. 24:24). These *antichrists* (*anti* means "against"; *christ* means "anointed one") are anointed either by themselves or by their followers to oppose Jesus's purposes. Jesus isn't the only one who warns that there will be many such opponents to him and his people during the end times.

The apostle John tells us in 1 John 2:18, "Dear children, this is the last hour; and as you have heard that the antichrist is coming, even now many antichrists have come. This is how we know it is the last hour" (NIV). John clearly says that his readers know that they're living in "the last hour" because *the* antichrist is coming, but he also informs us that throughout history, as in his day, there are "many antichrists" who oppose Jesus's purposes and exhibit the same evil qualities as *the* antichrist. It's not surprising, then, that there's a long list of world leaders whom Christians have thought were, or could be, this ultimate incarnation of evil.

The Roman emperor Nero or his successors. Many biblical scholars believe that Nero is the antichrist identified in the book of Revelation. Why? Because when his name in Greek is translated into Hebrew, the letters have the numeric value of 666—the mark of the beast (Rev. 13:18). Max J. Lee explains, "The best candidate is Emperor Nero, whose name transliterated into Hebrew *Neron Caesar (nrwn qsr)* adds up to 666. Nero infamously had Christians crucified, burnt alive, and torn alive by wild animals. Those with Nero's number would be citizens loyal to Rome."[1] Almost three centuries later, when the Great Persecution under the Roman emperor Diocletian shattered the church, many Christians assumed he was the first beast of Revelation 13 and that his successor, Caesar Galerius, was the second beast.[2] Two centuries after these assaults, some Christians identified another cruel emperor named Justinian as the antichrist.[3]

Pope Leo X: Because this pope opposed the Protestant Reformation and declared Martin Luther a heretic, the Reformer returned the favor and claimed that Pope Leo X was not the Vicar of Christ but rather the antichrist, Satan's representative on earth. Luther wrote,

> St. Paul calls Antichrist the man of sin and the son of perdition, because through his precepts and laws he will turn all the world from God and prevent God and the world from coming together; he shall be a master of sin and all iniquity, and yet will retain the name and appearance of Christ and call himself *Sanctimus* and *Vicarius Dei* and *Caput Ecclesiae* ["most holy one; vicar of God; head of the Church"], and persecute all who will not obey him. It is easy to recognize that the pope more than fits this description.[4]

Some Lutheran denominations still agree with Luther's assessment. For example, the doctrinal position of the Lutheran

Church—Missouri Synod states the following: "As to the Antichrist we teach that the prophecies of the Holy Scriptures concerning the Antichrist, 2 Thessalonians 2:3–12; 1 John 2:18, have been fulfilled in the Pope of Rome and his dominion."[5]

Robespierre or Napoleon. Many of those reading this book unconsciously think of antichrist possibilities only from a North American perspective. But there have been Christians in other parts of the world who have seen the Bible prophecies through other lenses—and with good cause. Maximilien Robespierre established his "Cult of the Supreme Being" after the French Revolution, and his opposition to Christ's cause was plain. He converted many Christian churches to places of worship for this new religion and even put a mountainous shrine to his political "god" in Notre Dame Cathedral.

When Robespierre ceremoniously descended from the shrine dressed in white, many Christians believed they were witnessing "the abomination of desolation" described in Daniel 9 and echoed in Jesus's prediction of Matthew 24:15 (see also Rev. 13:14). Since the abomination is some form of profane worship in God's temple, French Christians thought the final hour was upon them.

A few years later, when Napoleon's French army forcibly removed the pope from Rome in 1798, many Christians in colonial America thought this was a sign of the *end* of the end times. Many had been taught that the pope was the antichrist because he claimed to be the vicar (representative) of Christ on earth. Protestants considered the pope's rule over so much of Christendom the abomination of desolation—a profaning of the church worldwide. So when the pope was removed from power, these Christians believed they were witnessing the demise of the antichrist described in Daniel 7 and Revelation 13. Surely this meant the end of the world was near.

As these European events were observed by an increasingly churched population in the United States, an intense interest in the end times grew rapidly. The end-times excitement created a sense of urgency for missions and conversions that fueled the efforts of many churches in America at that time and continues to influence many churches in our time.

I will briefly add that the interest in the end times in America that was sparked by events related to France in the late eighteenth century was only heightened by Napoleon's later activities. His efforts at world domination combined with the bizarre natural calamities associated with the 1815 eruption of Mount Tambora, the most powerful volcano in human history,[6] made it seem to many that he had become the better candidate to fit the script for the antichrist.[7] This interpretation, too, gave many the sense that Christ's end-times prophecies were unfolding in imminent ways that demanded the urgent attention and activity of the church.

Adolf Hitler and his ilk. Not surprisingly, during World War II many people thought Adolf Hitler was the ultimate incarnation of the antichrist. He seemed to have demonic power to influence others, he fought to achieve world domination, and his atrocities against humanity were satanic, even though he claimed to be acting on divine authority. Hitler wrote in his book *Mein Kampf,* "I believe today that I am acting in the sense of the Almighty Creator. By warding off the Jews, I am fighting for the Lord's work."[8]

For Christians in the United States, Hitler readily comes to mind as an antichrist candidate because he was our enemy in World War II. Were we Christians in Russia, Lenin or Stalin might seem more plausible candidates because of their establishment of seventy years of an atheistic communist empire (reminiscent of the Babylonian captivity of Israel) that resulted in the death of millions of Russians and Eastern Europeans. These dictatorial rulers and their successors also converted churches to community centers or Communist Party headquarters while imprisoning or executing tens of thousands of Russian Orthodox priests and other Christian leaders.

After World War II, were we among the few Christians living in China we might have thought Mao Zedong was the antichrist.

His Cultural Revolution demanded the ejection of Western missionaries and the execution of countless thousands of people of faith. The cruelties actually rooted the commitments and fueled the amazing growth of the Chinese church as it exists in our time. Yet, despite Mao's massive crusade against faith, he was not the first antichrist candidate among Christians in China. Largely forgotten in China and in Western Christianity is the violent Taiping Rebellion in the 1850s led by a Christian convert who believed he could usher in the millennium by a revolt against the Chinese dynasty he considered the antichrist.[9]

Were we in the Middle East, where many of the world's oldest Christian communities have survived since the earliest days of the church, we might think of Saddam Hussein, who ruled Iraq (the site of ancient Babylon), as a modern antichrist. There is significant cause for such a conclusion. Hussein's atrocities were horrible beyond description. His overthrow and the subsequent related wars have resulted in the near extinction of ancient Christian communities throughout the Middle East. Such events might well lead us to think that it's time for Christ to establish his millennial kingdom to restore his people.

But others in the region had thought this previously. In the third century, Hippolytus, who was most likely Middle Eastern, opposed papal authority in Rome that he believed had compromised the church as it was predicted the antichrist would do. Hippolytus pushed the need for correction with the prediction that Christ would soon return to establish his kingdom. Based on a meticulous reading of the book of Daniel, Hippolytus calculated that Christ's birth was 5,500 years after creation and that the world would end 7,000 years after creation.[10] Various versions of this view were common for centuries, and Columbus actually used it to justify his New World voyages in 1492 so that the gospel would be preached "in all the world" prior to 1656—the time many thought Christ would return.[11]

Besides the dictatorial monsters of modern times, we might also think of those candidates for the antichrist that our forebears considered: King George III of England, who tried to rally his country's opposition to the American Revolution with religious prejudice by labeling it "the Presbyterian War"; Genghis Khan, who probably was responsible for the destruction of more governments, cities, faith centers, and people than anyone else in human history; or Sultan Mehmed II of the Ottoman Empire, who besieged Constantinople, the ancient center of Christianity that many considered to be the new Jerusalem, and breached its walls in 1453, allowing for the Muslim invasion of much of Christian Europe.

Mikhail Gorbachev and other Russian leaders. The recent death of the president of the former Soviet Union reminds us that he was identified as the antichrist by Robert W. Faid in his 1988 book *Gorbachev! Has the Real Antichrist Come?* Faid said, "The evidence is overwhelming that Gorbachev is the Antichrist," because he supposedly fulfilled fourteen of the sixteen prophecies about the antichrist in the book of Revelation.[12] Journalist Art Levine wrote a tongue-in-cheek article about Faid's claim titled "The Devil in Gorbachev," which begins by saying:

> Maybe it's that weird red mark on Mikhail Gorbachev's forehead. Maybe it's conservative disappointment that Ronald Reagan has gone to Moscow. But for whatever reason, there is a small but vocal group of fundamentalist Christians who are prepared to argue that the Soviet general secretary is the Antichrist, the Devil's agent on Earth. They don't simply mean that Gorbachev is an evil man, or that he represents an evil system. No. They mean that he is the tool of the Devil. The Antichrist. Mr. 666 himself.[13]

Despite Faid's confidence in his interpretation of the book of Revelation, Gorbachev failed to fully embody the magnitude and malice of the antichrist. This underscores the problem of trying to identify THE Antichrist: there are antichrists in every generation.

When Vladimir Putin invaded Ukraine on February 24, 2022, under the expressed spiritual purpose of reuniting the homelands of the Russian Orthodox Church, many Ukrainian, American, and European Christians began speculating that he could be the antichrist—and the potential instigator of a third world war that could also be Armageddon.[14]

US presidents. Finally, without providing too much embarrassing detail, those who have spent many years in American evangelicalism are well aware that a succession of American presidents have been proposed as the antichrist by their political opponents within the church. When John F. Kennedy's Roman Catholic affiliation was presumed to put the American presidency under the control of the pope, many evangelicals believed the end times had come. Some saw sufficient proof of evil to suspect the presence of the antichrist in Lyndon Johnson's Vietnam War explanations and efforts, the influence of Ronald Reagan's astrology-trusting wife, Nancy, Jimmy Carter's support of abortion, Bill Clinton's deceits, the Bushes' wars in the Middle East, Barack Obama's Muslim-sounding name, Donald Trump's character flaws, or Joe Biden's universal vaccination programs. In my own church, a Sunday school teacher rose to great prominence by comparing current events to end-times predictions, until the Sunday that he announced the president of the political party most dominant in our congregation was clearly *the* antichrist.

The Rebirth of Israel

Soon after Jesus lists the events that will accompany the end times, he also says that when he returns "on the clouds of heaven with power and great glory, . . . he will send out his angels with a loud trumpet call, and they will gather his elect from the four winds, from one end of heaven to the other" (Matt. 24:30–31). The idea that God will ultimately gather his people in one place from their dispersions throughout the world is a consistent biblical theme.

Since God made an "everlasting" promise to Abraham of a land for his people (Gen. 17:8) and also promised to restore his people to that land after their displacement (Jer. 16:15; Ezek. 20:34), few disagree that God promises to return the Jewish people to the promised land of Israel. But again, our understanding of how these prophecies are fulfilled depends on whether we take a near or far perspective.

Some Bible teachers think that these promises were fulfilled during biblical times, when God's people returned from slavery or exile. And clearly some Old Testament prophecies have been fulfilled by these historic returns (e.g., Isa. 44:26–45:1; Jer. 29:10–14). Still, other promises seem to relate to a return that's on a grander scale and is more tied to idyllic circumstances that will characterize the land of God's people as history culminates and the Messiah inaugurates his eternal kingdom (e.g., Isa. 11:6–11; Ezek. 20:41–44; 36:24–27; 37:21–28; Obad. 1:19–21).

Because of these latter passages, many Bible teachers believe the rebirth of the nation of Israel in the twentieth century is a key sign of the events leading to the culmination of the end times. Though the culmination is still in the future, these teachers believe the establishment of the state of Israel for the Jewish people in 1948 signals the nearness of Christ's return. They point to details from key Old Testament passages that speak of the regathering of God's people but were apparently not fulfilled by Old Testament circumstances (e.g., Deut. 30:3–10; Isa. 43:5–9; Ezek. 34:11–16; 36:24; 37:1–14). For many, these seemingly unfulfilled prophecies indicate that we should be anticipating Christ's return now.

We rejoice today that the nation of Israel is established and flourishing and that many Jewish people have returned to the promised land. But not all have returned, nor have all their hearts returned to God as was prophesied in certain passages (e.g., Jer. 31:23–34). So perhaps more events must unfold before the end of the end times. Or perhaps the idyllic words of these prophecies are exuberant expressions of what the Old Testament believers anticipated when they returned to the land from bondage and exile (Ps. 126). Or perhaps they are expressions of what God's people experience in the New Testament as he makes their hearts his dwelling place so that they are always in his land (2 Cor. 6:16; Eph. 3:17).

It's certainly reasonable and biblical to praise God's faithfulness and to anticipate Christ's return based on God's fulfillment of his promise to return his people to the promised land. Old Testament believers in dire circumstances clearly based much hope on this promise. New Testament believers are expected to do the same. Still, if we turn back the clock, there have been several times since the days of Jesus when Christians might have claimed the fulfillment of Old Testament prophecies about Israel's rebirth and the nearness of Christ's return. Let me mention a few.

The Year 1099. During the eleventh century, Christians in Jerusalem were being persecuted by the city's Islamic rulers. In response, Pope Urban II called for a crusade to help these Eastern Christians and to recapture the Holy Land. On June 7, 1099, the Crusaders reached Jerusalem. By July 14 they penetrated "the defenses, and the Gate of Saint Stephen was opened. The rest of the knights and soldiers then poured in, the city was captured, and tens of thousands of its occupants were slaughtered. The crusaders had achieved their aims, and Jerusalem was in Christian hands."[15]

Of course, from the standpoint of those who did not see New Testament believers as those engrafted by faith into God's covenant with the Jews (see Rom. 9:25–26; 11:17–24; Gal. 3:7–9, 29), the Crusaders' victory wasn't a fulfillment of Old Testament promises to the *Jewish* people. As a consequence, many of those killed by the Crusaders were the Jewish occupants of the city. Still, Pope Urban II and much of Christendom would have viewed this event as a fulfillment of God's plan for his people.

The Years 1917–18. On November 2, 1917, England's foreign secretary, Arthur James Balfour, wrote a letter to Baron Lionel Walter Rothschild, Great Britain's most prominent Jewish citizen and a strong supporter of the establishment of a new nation of Israel.

In the letter he stated that "His Majesty's Government [would] view with favor the establishment in Palestine of a national home for the Jewish people, and will use their best endeavors to facilitate the achievement of this object."[16] This letter became known as the Balfour Declaration, and many Bible-believing Christians see this as the trigger for end-times events.

Because of the Balfour Declaration, on December 9, 1917, British troops pushed back the Ottoman army guarding Jerusalem, and two days later General Edmund Allenby marched triumphantly into the Old City. He went on to defeat the Ottoman army at what he deliberately called "the battle of Megiddo," even though only a small portion of the battle was fought there, in order to tie his actions to biblical prophecy. As you may know, the Hebrew word *Armageddon* (see Rev. 16:16) literally means "hill of Megiddo."

Following World War I and the Treaty of Versailles, Great Britain was given the responsibility of administering the area known as Palestine, leading to the establishment of modern Israel. One of Israel's prime ministers, Benjamin Netanyahu, made the direct connection to the Balfour Declaration, stating that this provision for Jewish people was "a central milestone" in establishing his nation.[17] Indeed it was, but whether it was the fulfillment of biblical promises for the restoration of Israel prior to the second coming, or only a precursor, or merely another chapter in the troubled history of an embattled region of the world, is a matter Bible scholars debate.

The Year 1948. On May 14, 1948, David Ben-Gurion, Israel's first prime minister, declared the establishment of a Jewish state known as the *Land* of Israel (Eretz-Israel). The next day the neighboring Arab states of Egypt, Transjordan, and Syria, along with Palestinian Arabs, invaded Israel. According to the US Department of State,

> Though the United Nations brokered two cease-fires during the conflict, fighting continued into 1949. Israel and the Arab states did not reach any formal armistice agreements until February. Under

49

separate agreements between Israel and the neighboring states of Egypt, Lebanon, Transjordan, and Syria, these bordering nations agreed to formal armistice lines. Israel gained some territory formerly granted to Palestinian Arabs under the United Nations resolution in 1947. Egypt and Jordan retained control over the Gaza Strip and the West Bank respectively.[18]

Many students of prophecy believed this reestablishment of the land of promise for the people of Israel was a highly significant sign of the nearness of the end times. One prominent author even predicted that the Lord would return in 1988—forty years after Israel's occupation of the Holy Land—reflecting the "generation" of time Jesus spoke of in Matthew 24:34 (more on this prediction in chap. 5).

June 5–10, 1967. This brief conflict, known as the Six-Day War or the Arab-Israeli War, allowed Israel to capture the Sinai Peninsula, Gaza Strip, West Bank, Old City of Jerusalem, and Golan Heights. Some Christians today view that series of battles as a more complete fulfillment of biblical prophecy about the return of Jews to their homeland that's to precede the coming of the Messiah. In an article titled "Almost Armageddon: Why the Six-Day War Was a Prophetic Milestone," Joel Rosenberg is quoted as saying, "Throughout the Old Testament, God says that He is going to draw the Jewish people back to the land. . . . For 4,000 years people have wanted [Jerusalem] and they have fought hard to get it. And so, the fact that Israel controls it today is biblical, it's prophetic."[19]

Wars and rumors of wars in and about the promised land, antichrist candidates across centuries and countries, and Israel's repeated rebirths have affirmed biblical prophecy but have also created questions about which prophecies have been confirmed and which are yet to be fulfilled. How do we measure history to know if the events before us and about us are propelling us nearer to the end of the end times? That is the subject of the next chapter.

3

Views of Previous Times

In the previous chapter we considered the impact of having a near or far view of prophetic fulfillment regarding only a few end-times issues: wars related to the Holy Land, the identity of the antichrist, and the significance of the rebirth of modern Israel. Of course, there are many more issues people ponder when considering what they have heard about the last days, including:

- Does the Old Testament temple need to be rebuilt before Jesus returns?
- Will Jesus's return be preceded by a single world government?
- Will Jesus's return be preceded by a single monetary system for the whole world?
- Will every person have a government ID or mark prior to or during the abominations of the antichrist?

- Will Jesus physically descend to the Mount of Olives at his second coming?
- How will all the nations of the earth see Jesus when he returns?
- Must ethnic Jews be evangelized before Jesus returns?
- Must the gospel be preached to all people groups before Jesus returns?
- Do all people groups need to have the Bible in their own language before Christ returns?
- Does Christ return once or twice or more?
- Will there be a great tribulation?
- Will believers go through the great tribulation?
- Will Russia, China, a coalition of Arab nations, or a coalition of all nations fight against God's people at the battle of Armageddon?
- Will angels join in the final battle between good and evil?
- Could Jesus come tomorrow—or today?
- When Jesus comes back, is that the end of this world, or does he spend a thousand years reigning over the earth before establishing the new heaven and new earth?

As I compiled this list of questions, many possible answers swirled in my brain and a few more definite thoughts crossed my mind. First, I'm sure that a few readers are certain that they have an answer for each of these questions. Second, I'm also sure that most readers think there's no way they'll ever be able to answer these questions. Yet those of us raised in evangelical churches have heard such questions debated by informed, godly, and well-intentioned Bible teachers throughout our lives.

To claim the hope that the Bible says its prophecies were meant to inspire, we shouldn't just shrug our shoulders and say, "They don't matter because no one knows for sure." God gave the prophecies for a reason, and our faith isn't adequately supported without understanding the essentials of his plans for our future. We should know, however, that there are different perspectives about biblical prophecy that give rise to such interesting questions but will also help us determine the answers to our essential questions.

When we understand the key ideas that form those perspectives, then we'll understand why some choose near or far interpretations of specific biblical prophecies. More importantly, we'll be able to look beyond the blizzard of questions to the biblical truths behind them that unite and strengthen our hearts. Our differences are distractions if they undermine our confidence in the truth of Scripture or our ability to see how it gives us definite hope for today and needed strength for tomorrow.

Three Views of Biblical History

One of the reasons godly people vary in how they interpret biblical prophecy is that they view biblical history differently. These differences largely revolve around the ways they think God deals with his people in the Old and New Testaments. The distinctions I'm about to explain will have very little nuance in order to make the differences clear because I want everyone to understand the lenses (or filters) they may be using as they look at different Bible passages. Still, I confess that these explanations are simplified and may be less refined than sophisticated scholars would prefer.

Lutheran

How does looking back at biblical history affect how we look forward through biblical prophecy? One answer will become immediately evident to readers who come from traditional Lutheran backgrounds. Martin Luther broke with the Roman Catholic Church over a disagreement about whether human merit based on keeping God's commands or church traditions could make us right with God. As a result, the Reformer definitely had an un-favorable view of how Old Testament laws and worship require-ments could apply to us.

Luther wanted those in his church to be very clear about the dif-ference between the law (Old Testament commands) and the gos-pel (New Testament grace). He believed that the law and the gospel needed to work in concert to drive us to the grace of Christ. The law would kill with its demands, and the gospel would make alive with its provision. Still, the law wasn't the gospel and was not the focus of Christ or his church. A simple representation of Luther's view looks like this:

Law ≠ Gospel

But if the contents of the law are not the gospel for us today, what do we do with all those prophecies that are included in the law portions of the Old Testament? Luther didn't ignore them. Rather, he believed the focus of the Old Testament prophecies wasn't a plan for Israel but preparation for the New Testament gospel. The prophecies were important not because they predicted something for the Old Testament people (i.e., people mired in the law) but because they portrayed how Christ was coming to rescue the church (i.e., people of grace) from any form of human legal-ism. Since Jews were people of the law, Jewish preservation or the rebirth of a Jewish nation were not God's primary focus. The prophecies of the Old Testament were chiefly meant to highlight Christ's rescue of the church from the shackles of the law and the antichrist (i.e., Roman Catholic legalisms and the pope, as Luther understood things).

Luther believed himself to be part of this rescue through his world- and perspective-changing ministry that was focused on how we're made right with God by grace alone. Luther saw his Reformation ministry as the light of the gospel breaking into the darkness of a millennia of tribulation, which he understood to be the Ottoman Empire's influences over the Holy Land and its subsequent invasion of Europe, as well as a longer period of gospel suppression through Roman Catholic domination of the Christian world.

This perspective confirmed in Luther's mind that the Jews were incidental to the purposes of biblical prophecy, that the pope was the antichrist, and—since the antichrist had already come in the person of the pope—that the climax of the end times was near and Christ would come very soon.[1]

Few of us would fault Luther for his focus on salvation by grace and not by works (see, e.g., Eph. 2:8–9). Still, it's important to see how one who is so right on gospel essentials might come to very different conclusions from many modern evangelicals (and many modern Lutherans) on significant end-times specifics. Luther's view of how biblical history was unfolding affected how he saw biblical prophecy applying.

Dispensational

A view held by many people in Bible-believing churches today is reminiscent of some aspects of Luther's perspective regarding the significance of the Old Testament for us. Yet this view comes to very different conclusions about how the prophecies of that period apply to Jews and to us. More than three centuries after Luther, a man named John Nelson Darby advanced a view that perceived God dealing with his people in the Old Testament far differently than he does in the New Testament. This view developed into the teaching we now identify as Dispensationalism.[2] Darby and traditional Dispensationalists teach that biblical history unfolds through a series of time periods, called dispensations, in which God tests the obedience of humanity in different ways.

According to Dispensationalism, God dealt with Jewish people of the Old Testament in significantly different ways from how he deals with the rest of us today. This means God has separate programs for Israel and the New Testament church. One simple way to represent this view looks like this:

OT | NT

The separation between the Old and New Testaments indicated in this little graphic represents the separate plans that God has for how he relates to his people. In the Old Testament, God tested his people's obedience through different dispensations of holy standards that had different expectations and provisions. In the New Testament, he relates to his people through their faith in the full revelation of grace that has been made apparent through Jesus Christ. The ways that the Old Testament dispensations led into the church age are represented in the more detailed chart in figure 3.1.

Although God tested his people in different ways in the various dispensations, it's important for Dispensationalists to affirm that God never annulled his promises to Israel. God's promises to Abraham are eternal (Gen. 17:3–8). To the extent that those promises didn't materialize in the Old Testament, they have yet to be fulfilled

Figure 3.1
Dispensational View of the Bible

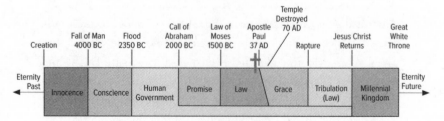

God reveals his salvation plan through successive "dispensations," periods of time when humanity is tested in some respect of obedience—followed by disobedience and judgment—in order that the necessity of God's plan of salvation by grace would be cumulatively revealed.

in the age(s) to come. So, unlike Luther, Dispensational scholars teach that God still has a plan for Israel that's described in the end-times prophecies of the Old Testament. Consequently, the fulfillment of these Old Testament prophecies is chronologically far removed from their origin, though it may now be very near to us as we see ancient prophecies coming to light in current events like the rebirth of the nation of Israel. What's critical for accurate interpretation, according to Dispensationalists, is that Old Testament prophecies be applied to those to whom they were given: the people of Israel—that is, Jews.

The prophecies that relate to those of us in the New Testament church are those given in the New Testament or are the spillover effect of what God promised for Jews in the Old Testament. "Spillover" is probably not an adequate way of expressing all the dimensions of this thought, but I mean for it to communicate how intertwined are the national, international, and eternal implications of God's care for his covenant people. What affects Israel affects the church, even if the prophecies being fulfilled most directly apply to Israel. For example, if mass conversion of Jews is a precursor to the final events of this world, then the efforts to convert them affect the plans and people of the church.

Covenantal

A third perspective on biblical history that has implications for either near or far interpretations of biblical prophecy is the Covenantal view. Like Dispensational advocates, Covenantal supporters see God's plan for his people unfolding in a series of eras that vary in how God expresses his care. What distinguishes the Covenantal view from the Lutheran and Dispensational perspectives is the understanding that each of the eras has the same foundation: grace.

In the successive eras of biblical history, which are marked by a series of covenants, God is unfolding the progressive implications of the very first prophecy in the Bible (Gen. 3:15). There he promised to send a Redeemer to rescue his people from their corrupted hearts and world. By that first prophecy, God made clear two things: (1) he would send an offspring from the lineage of Adam and Eve who would crush the influence of Satan; and (2) all humanity would need that Redeemer. None of us are our Redeemer. God's rescue requires God's provision.

Nothing in any era following that first promise of Jesus's redeeming work could undermine God's initial declaration that no human effort would ever be sufficient for our rescue from sin. In fact, each succeeding covenant, whereby God advances plans for his dealings with his people, reveals more dimensions of the nature and necessity of divine grace. See a more detailed description of a Covenantal view of biblical history in figure 3.2.

In the covenant with Adam, God establishes his unconditional and undeserved creation *provision*. Through Noah, God promises flawed humanity his *preservation* of a corrupted world. In the covenant with Abraham, he promises *multiplication* of the blessings of faith for all nations. Through Moses, God provides deliverance

Figure 3.2
Covenantal View of the Bible

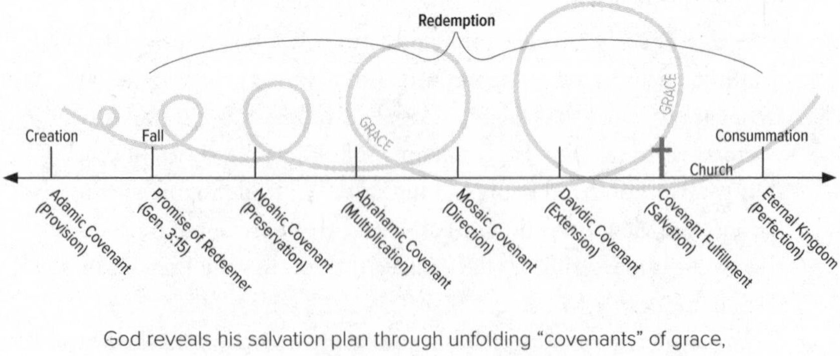

God reveals his salvation plan through unfolding "covenants" of grace, individual promises of divine provision that *progressively* and *increasingly* reveal the nature and necessity of redeeming grace that culminates in the ministry of Jesus Christ.

from bondage and *direction* for living with his blessing. In the covenant with David, God promises the *extension* of his rule to universal and eternal dimensions. In Christ, all the blessings of our *salvation* culminate in accord with the grace God has been revealing since his dealings with humanity began.

Each covenant differs from the others in some ways, but all are built on the grace in which God's people would need to trust until it culminates in the person and work of Jesus. An image for relating a Covenantal perspective looks like this:

<u>Law → Gospel</u>
Grace

The law as expressed in the Old Testament leads to the gospel as revealed in the New Testament, with all of biblical history built on the foundation of God's grace. The different ways God's people learned to depend on grace through his unfolding covenants led them forward to understand the necessity of faith in Jesus (Gal. 3:26), who is the ultimate fulfillment of the promises God initiated through his covenants.

This perspective doesn't put the law in opposition to the gospel but prepares all people in all times to depend on God's grace. The law is gracious because God uses it to direct us in a good and safe path for life and because it teaches us how much we need God's grace when we fail to follow the law. So the gospel of Jesus Christ in the New Testament isn't a different path to salvation but the destination that God's Old Testament law requires, which Jesus fulfills (Matt. 5:17; Gal. 3:24). This means that grace unfolds in all of Scripture, and its dimensions are getting clearer and more powerful through the successive covenants. That's why the spiral line representing the grace of God expands over time in figure 3.2.

The implication of grace unfolding throughout Scripture is that Covenantal theologians don't think the Old Testament and its prophecies relate only to Jews. The promises God made to his people are instructive for all who depend on Jesus and expect him to return to rescue us from this present evil world. Covenantal theologians see the fulfillment of some Old and New Testament prophecies as relating to only Jews when the Bible specifies that, but they also think many biblical prophecies can relate to God's people across the total sweep of biblical history (e.g., Gen. 17:4–5; 18:18; Pss. 22:27; 64:9; 86:9). They don't automatically rule out the Old Testament prophets' ability or desire to predict events for New Testament Christians, since all nations are meant to see how grace alone claims God's people for eternity. So some prophecies relate to the past, some to the present, and some to the future—events near and far.

Of course, there are more views of biblical history than I have covered in these few pages, but these three views—Lutheran, Dispensational, and Covenantal—are large enough buckets to hold most of the end-times teaching in Bible-believing churches today. Let's be clear that each perspective is held by genuine believers. Yes, different views of how biblical history unfolds affect how people understand the ways that God will fulfill biblical prophecy. We need to know this background to understand why there are different views on the end times. Still, we need to remember that all the views we have considered hold that we're saved by grace through faith in the shed blood and resurrection victory of Jesus Christ. We need to start on that common ground or we'll approach the next discussion with inappropriate suspicion of or separation from brothers and sisters in Christ.

If someone takes a near view on a particular prophecy that I interpret with a far view, then we might have a sincere debate about who's right. If the debate is serious enough, we might even think that people shouldn't listen to the other person. But that doesn't mean we just assume the other person doesn't believe the Bible, doesn't have faith in God's grace, or doesn't believe that Jesus is coming back.

Four Views of the Millennium

So then, if we all believe the Bible is true, Jesus is our Savior, and our Savior is coming back for his people, how do our views of biblical history affect our understanding of the future? Suddenly we are back to that question of whether many biblical prophecies are about things near to the time and place of their writing, far from that time and place, or some mix of these alternatives. The choices we make about these matters can have dramatic implications for our views of end-times events, when they happen, and in what order. We will discuss these in later chapters.

For now, it's important to know that the four most common views Bible-believing Christians hold and debate about the end times have the word *millennial* in their names. When Christians talk about THE millennium, they're usually referring to the thousand-year reign of Christ spoken of in Revelation 20:4: "They came to life and reigned with Christ for a thousand years." The question we debate with such rigor in the church is this: Is that millennium near or far or some mix of those alternatives? How you answer will inevitably be linked to one of the views of biblical history already discussed—even if no one ever told you that.

We all have (and rightly so) a context for how we read Scripture, and the context of biblical history in which we place the thousand years of Revelation 20:4 will determine our view of the timing and significance of that text and the many biblical prophecies related to it. That millennial era is critical to which of the four main views we use to view the big picture of the end times:

1. Dispensational Premillennial
2. Historic Premillennial
3. Amillennial
4. Postmillennial

Here's a quick explanation: The prefixes *pre-* ("before") and *post-* ("after") refer to whether Jesus will return *before* or *after* the millennium. A *Dispensational* Premillennial view holds that Jesus will return *before* the millennium and interprets many related prophecies according to the Dispensational view of biblical history (see figure 3.1). *Historic* Premillennial advocates also believe that Jesus will come before the millennium, but they usually hold to the Covenantal view of history (see figure 3.2). This basically means that Dispensational Premillennialists have much more to say about how specific prophecies are tied to Israel than do Historic Premillennialists, who relate much more to God's plans for the worldwide church.

Amillennialists and Postmillennialists also tend to view biblical history from a Covenantal perspective. The prefix *a-* ("without") is somewhat misleading, since it could wrongly imply that this viewpoint teaches that Bible prophecies don't include a millennium. Amillennial advocates actually believe we're already in the *spiritual* realities of the millennium. There's a sense in which Postmillennialists also believe that we're already in the millennium, but they define it as a time of gradual improvement of *earthly* realities that leads to a golden age of blessing prior to Christ's second coming, which probably is really far in the future.

All four views are held by godly Christians who have searched the Scriptures before forming their conclusions. The Covenantal views have been held by Bible-trusting believers for centuries. The Dispensational view is relatively new but probably is held by more people today. The advocates of each view certainly think theirs is the most consistent with Scripture. No one is trying to make us disregard the Bible or doubt that Jesus is returning.

This book won't try to persuade you that one view is more biblical than the others. Instead, it will give you enough information to understand key features of each view, the faith that each affirms, and the hope that all believers share through God's certain promises for the last days.

4

Dispensational Premillennial View

Many people learned about the Dispensational Premillennial view of the last days through the enormously
popular Left Behind series by Jerry Jenkins and Tim
LaHaye. The first book in the series begins aboard an airborne
Boeing 747 heading to London. Suddenly, without warning, some
of the passengers mysteriously vanish from their seats. The book
grabs our attention with its alarming details: "Terror and chaos
slowly spread not only through the plane but also worldwide as
unusual events continue to unfold. For those who have been left
behind, the apocalypse has just begun. In one cataclysmic moment, millions around the globe disappear. Vehicles, suddenly un-
manned, careen out of control. People are terror stricken as loved
ones vanish before their eyes."[1]

The bestselling Left Behind series introduced millions of readers
to the Dispensational view of the future along with its key events
and concepts, including the rapture, the tribulation, the antichrist,

Figure 4.1

Dispensational Premillennial View of the End Times

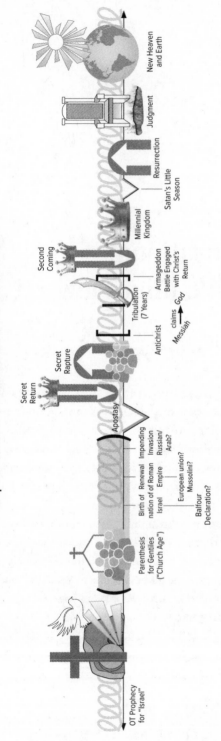

Parenthetical "church age" interrupts the fulfillment of prophetic prediction prior to continued unfolding of God's kingdom purposes.

the battle of Armageddon, and the millennium—each of which we'll explore in this and following chapters.

My guess is that many of you reading this book either were raised in churches that taught the Dispensational Premillennial view or were exposed to it through books like the Left Behind series or Hal Lindsey's bestselling *The Late Great Planet Earth*. I grew up in churches that embraced this view, and my lay preacher father loved his Scofield Reference Bible, which articulates this perspective in study notes sprinkled throughout the text. We attended prophecy conferences, where speakers showed highly detailed diagrams that revealed the sequence of events leading up to the rapture, the tribulation, and the other key end-times events. The graphics must have made a lasting impression on me because I feel the need to use similar charts in this book to help you visualize what I'm describing.[2]

What Is Dispensationalism?

The first key feature of traditional Dispensationalism is that it divides human history into distinct periods of time called "dispensations." The original Scofield Reference Bible offers this explanation: "A dispensation is a period of time during which man is tested in respect of obedience to some specific revelation of the will of God. Seven such dispensations are distinguished in Scripture."[3] If you look back at figure 3.1 in the previous chapter, you'll see that those seven dispensations that precede the millennium are Innocence, Conscience, Human Government, Promise, Law, Grace, and Tribulation. Then comes the Millennial Kingdom that will last one thousand years. You should note that several of these dispensations overlap, but there are plans for how God will secure the eternity of people in the different dispensations that do *not* overlap. This non-overlap of salvation plans will be discussed more in depth later in this chapter and in chapters to come.

The second key feature of traditional Dispensationalism is that God has two separate and distinct programs for rescuing people from the corruptions of this world: one for Israel and another for the church. Daniel P. Fuller states, "The basic premise of Dispensationalism is two purposes God expressed in the formation of two peoples who maintain their distinction throughout eternity."[4] Faithful Jews and non-Jewish believers worship the same God, but he has separate plans for their futures. Ethnic Israel and gentile believers follow different paths to different destinies. This is seen not as an anti-Semitic prejudice concocted by modern preachers but as God's commitment to fulfill promises he made to Israel through his Old Testament prophets.

To understand how Dispensationalists interpret the prophets, we need a third important Dispensational distinctive. Dispensationalists claim that if Old Testament prophecies are interpreted literally rather than symbolically, they fully support this view of distinctly different plans for Israel and the church. So, from a Dispensational perspective, non-Dispensationalists too often take literal promises to Israel and make them figures of speech relating spiritual truths to God's people in general. Because these representational or symbolic interpretations don't seem to make clear God's distinct plans for Jews, Dispensationalists think that God's faithfulness to his Word is put in question by non-Dispensationalists.

Old Testament Interpretation

Clarifying what is meant by a *literal* interpretation of Scripture is important. All the views in this book will be based on what their advocates believe is a literal interpretation of the Bible. By literal we all mean the interpretation that's most true to the literary intention of the author. For example, no one—including a Dispensationalist—believes that the lamb seated upon the throne in Revelation 7:17 is a woolly creature with four legs and a bleating voice. It's Jesus.

All Bible-believing Christians know that we must use the literary context of a Scripture passage to determine whether its words are a direct reference to an object, person, or idea, or if the words contain metaphors or symbols. None of us think we can determine meaning with a wooden, nonliterary understanding of how words communicate. When the psalmist refers to God as "the rock of my salvation," we don't think he intended to tell us that our Lord is made of stone.

Charles Ryrie, one of the chief voices for Dispensationalism, explains that "the literal meaning of words is the normal approach to their understanding in all languages. It might also be designated the plain interpretation so that no one receives the mistaken notion that the literal principle rules out figures of speech. Symbols, figures of speech, and types are all interpreted plainly in this method, and they are in no way contrary to literal interpretation."[5]

Though there's much agreement on what literal interpretation should be, Dispensationalists think non-Dispensationalists depart from the literal method when they interpret Old Testament prophecies related to Israel. Ryrie acknowledges "that the nondispensationalist is a literalist in much of his interpretation of the Scriptures but charges him with allegorizing or spiritualizing when it comes to the interpretation of prophecy. The dispensationalist claims to be consistent in his use of this principle, and he accuses the nondispensationalist of being inconsistent in his use of it."[6]

The particular inconsistency that most concerns Dispensationalists is taking words specifically addressed to God's chosen people in the Old Testament era and applying them to other people who become part of the church in the New Testament age. This difference isn't about what a figure of speech means but about which persons are being addressed.

Floyd Hamilton, an Amillennialist, acknowledges the interpretation that would result if he and other non-Dispensationalists consistently applied the literal method as the Dispensationalists desire: "Now we must frankly admit that a literal interpretation of the Old Testament prophecies gives us just such a picture of an earthly reign of the Messiah as the premillennialist [i.e., Dispensational Premillennialist] pictures. That was the kind of Messianic kingdom that the Jews of the time of Christ were looking for, on the basis of a literal kingdom interpretation of the Old Testament promises."[7]

From the apostles' own expectations prior to Christ's crucifixion, we know that the Jews were looking for a Messianic kingdom in which Israel would have unprecedented and eternal prosperity, power, and peace. They based their expectations on God's promises through their prophets (e.g., Isa. 11; Jer. 33; Mic. 4). Traditional Dispensationalists believe that prior to Jesus's resurrection the apostles were wrong about the timing of the Messianic kingdom but right about its nature. These promises to Israel in the Old Testament, including the prophecies about the restoration of Israel, don't apply to the church. They were literally given to Israel and are literally intended for Israel.

Old Testament Confirmation

How do Dispensationalists arrive at this conclusion that the Old Testament promises to Israel are limited to Israel? One of the key passages for answering this question is Daniel 9. In the context of that chapter, Daniel and the people of Israel are being held captive in Babylon. Then Daniel reads Jeremiah's earlier prophecy, stating that Israel's captivity would last only seventy years (Jer. 25:11–12; 29:10). Since the captivity has already extended almost that long, Daniel realizes the fulfillment of Jeremiah's prophecy is near. So Daniel prays to the Lord, asking him to forgive Israel's sins, return the Jews to their land, and restore both Jerusalem and the temple.

In response to Daniel's prayer, the Lord sends the angel Gabriel to give Daniel wisdom and insight about Israel's future. The angel says to Daniel, "Seventy weeks [lit. 'sevens'] are decreed about your people and your holy city, to finish the transgression, to put an end to sin, and to atone for iniquity, to bring in everlasting righteousness, to seal both vision and prophet, and to anoint a most holy place" (Dan. 9:24). Dispensational scholars interpret the "weeks" or "sevens" to represent periods of seven years that will be multiplied seventy times (70 × 7 = 490 years) for the prophecy's fulfillment.

That means almost five hundred years will pass before the ultimate fulfillment of Gabriel's words to Daniel is realized. That's long beyond the seventy years prophesied by Jeremiah. Also, Gabriel speaks of an atonement for iniquity that will "bring in everlasting righteousness." That's a result far beyond Daniel's immediate expectation and far beyond the spiritual state of Israel when they return to the promised land after their captivity.

In other words, instead of focusing on the end of Israel's exile in Babylon, Gabriel's prophecy seems to jet much further into the future, describing the ultimate fulfillment of God's promises to Israel—including an end of transgression and sin, atonement for sin, restoration of the temple ("the most holy place"), and the establishment of "everlasting righteousness."

Since Gabriel seems to speak of events well into the future, Daniel and his readers will surely want to know the time frame of that prophecy. Interpreting it correctly will also require knowing when the 490-year period begins. So Gabriel elaborates:

> Know therefore and understand that from the going out of the word to restore and build Jerusalem to the coming of an anointed one, a prince, there shall be seven weeks. Then for sixty-two weeks it shall be built again with squares and moat, but in a troubled time. And after the sixty-two weeks, an anointed one shall be cut off and shall have nothing. And the people of the prince who is to come shall destroy the city and the sanctuary. Its end shall come with a flood, and to the end there shall be war. Desolations are decreed. And he shall make a strong covenant with many for one week, and for half of the week he shall put an end to sacrifice and offering. And on the wing of abominations shall come one who makes desolate, until the decreed end is poured out on the desolator. (Dan. 9:25–27)

Gabriel says the starting point for the 490-year period will be "from the going out of the word to restore and rebuild Jerusalem." Although we can identify three or four possible dates when a pagan king issued a decree to release Jewish captives to restore and rebuild Jerusalem, leading Dispensationalists such as John Walvoord and Dr. David Jeremiah believe that the most likely date is 445 BC. That's when some scholars say the pagan king Artaxerxes gave the Jewish exiles permission to return to their homeland (Neh. 2:1).[8] So Artaxerxes's proclamation would mark the starting date for the 490 years of Gabriel's prophecy.

Notice, then, that Gabriel divides the 490 years into three parts. The first part lasts seven weeks (49 years, if we keep interpreting each week as a period of seven years) and is the time between the decree to rebuild Jerusalem and its completion. The second part lasts 62 sevens (434 years), and at the end of that period "an anointed one [Greek: *Christos*] shall be cut off [i.e., put to death]." So the time from the decree to rebuild Jerusalem until the death of an anointed one is 483 years.

Accepting this timing can result in calculations that coincide precisely and wonderfully with the crucifixion of Jesus Christ. The organization Jews for Jesus connects the dots, stating that "Jesus of Nazareth was born into the Jewish world and proclaimed his messiahship 483 years after the decree to rebuild and restore Jerusalem was issued. In the year 30 C.E., Jesus was executed by crucifixion."[9] So, according to Dispensationalists, the first two parts of Daniel's amazing prophecy have been accurately fulfilled.[10]

But what about the third part—the final week? Gabriel says that after the 62-week period that culminates in the death of an anointed one, then a destroying prince "shall make a strong covenant with many for one week." One more week of years is needed to complete Gabriel's prophecy. This means God's kingdom of "everlasting righteousness" that the prophets predicted and the Jews expected should have followed seven years after Christ's crucifixion. That didn't happen. So what happened?

The Church Age

Traditional Dispensationalists tell us that the 490-year prophetic stopwatch that had counted down from 445 BC to Jesus's crucifixion ceased ticking with only seven years left on the watch. Why? Because the church age—a parenthetical time unforeseen by the prophets and excluded from their prophecies—had begun (see figure 4.1). Up to that point in time, God had been focusing his salvation plan on the nation of Israel, not the gentiles. But when Israel rejected their Messiah—the "anointed one" mentioned in Daniel 9—God turned his attention

A Stopwatch Perspective

to building the church in an unexpected and unprophesied period. Dispensationalists call this "the great parenthesis." In this period the ticks on the prophetic stopwatch don't move forward, and they won't until God's promises to Israel reengage at the end of the church age.

This doesn't mean that God has abandoned his plan for Israel. The promises of God are irrevocable (Rom. 11:26–29). Instead, Dispensationalists teach that God widened his mercy by doing what was unexpected—making the glories of his grace available to gentiles through the church (11:25). The church doesn't replace Israel but is the beneficiary of its failure to embrace the Savior who now offers his mercy to all nations. The prophetic stopwatch can start ticking again for Israel (most Dispensationalists think God has already started it). But until then God is on the unforeseen, unexpected, and unanticipated mission of extending his grace to all people through the ministries of the church of Jesus Christ in this age of parenthesis. Note how the spiraling line representing God's *prophesied* grace in figure 4.1 stops as the church age begins and doesn't start again until its latter stages.

Dispensationalists believe the apostle Paul describes God's unforeseen dealings with the church as the "mystery" of the gospel in Ephesians 3:2–6:

71

Surely you have heard about the administration of God's grace that was given to me for you, that is, the mystery made known to me by revelation, as I have already written briefly. In reading this, then, you will be able to understand my insight into the mystery of Christ, which was not made known to people in other generations as it has now been revealed by the Spirit to God's holy apostles and prophets. This mystery is that through the gospel the Gentiles are heirs together with Israel, members together of one body, and sharers together in the promise in Christ Jesus. (NIV)

In this case, Dispensationalists say, a mystery isn't something un-solved but something unanticipated. God's extending the gospel to the gentiles befuddles the Jews because they understood the Old Tes-tament prophecies to be about and for them. They never anticipated God's mercy would extend so far. This doesn't make the spread of the gospel of grace wrong but gloriously mysterious. Still, the blessings of this mystery shouldn't be blurred with God's promises to Israel.

According to Dispensationalists, even though the church in-cludes both Jewish and gentile believers, the church should never be confused with Israel. The church began at Pentecost and has been the focus of God's attention for the last two thousand years. Israel was established much earlier and is not the church. The church doesn't receive the blessings intended for Israel. But if God's pro-gram for Israel remains separate from his program for the church, then how will the prophetic stopwatch for Israel ever start ticking again to fulfill the final seven years of Daniel's prophecy? The answer is not a mystery, but it is a secret—a secret that Dispensa-tionalists believe the New Testament reveals to us.

The Secret Rapture of the Church

What is this secret all about? To answer that from a Dispensational perspective, we have to step back to the late eighteenth and early nineteenth centuries. The horrific events surrounding the French Revolution combined with a string of natural disasters sparked global interest in the topic of the end times. So, in the 1830s the world was ripe for receiving the teachings of a man named John Nelson Darby, who believed that the Bible taught a "secret rapture" of the church that would rescue believers from the world's evils.

The word *rapture* isn't in the Bible but comes from a Latin word meaning "caught up." Darby believed the rapture would involve Jesus returning to earth to "catch up" or "snatch up" believers with him into the air to provide a way of escape from a time of great tribulation. So, no matter how bad things seemed to be getting, Christians could take hope in knowing they would be rescued from the worst of the world's evil.

The "desolations" that Daniel describes in the final week of years prior to the end of Gabriel's prophecy seemed to characterize this tribulation period. So Darby concluded that the rapture must come before the tribulation, which immediately precedes the final coming of Christ when he establishes his kingdom of "everlasting righteousness." The rapture is called "secret" for at least three reasons: (1) no one will see this first coming of Jesus during the end times except believers, in contrast to his final coming after the tribulation when "every eye will see him" (Rev. 1:7); (2) it will result in the inexplicable disappearance of Christians from society; and (3) the apostle Paul refers to the rapture as "a mystery" because it hadn't previously been revealed to either Old Testament believers or the church (1 Cor. 15:51).

Popular books and movies tend to focus on the sensational aspects of this secret nature of the rapture: pilots disappearing from planes, doctors disappearing from surgeries, and least likely saints taken skyward with hypocritical preachers left behind. Dr. Tim LaHaye describes this understanding of the rapture in ways that have captured the imagination of many:

> When more than one-half of a billion people suddenly depart this earth, leaving their earthly belongings behind, pandemonium and confusion will certainly reign for a time.

A million conversations will end midsentence.

A million phones . . . will suddenly go dead.

A woman will reach for a man's hand in the dark . . . and no one will be there. . . .

A mother will pull back the covers in a bassinet, smelling the sweet baby smell one moment but suddenly kissing empty space and looking into empty blankets.[11]

The shock and awe on the earth that accompany this secret rapture tend to grab popular attention, but for those most concerned with understanding the end times from a Dispensational perspective, the snatching up of Christians into the air is what's most important. Because the church will be raptured with Jesus, God can reengage his program for Israel. Dr. David Jeremiah explains the nature and importance of the secret rapture:

I believe there will be two-stages to the second coming of Christ. First, He will come suddenly in the air to snatch up His own. This is the Rapture, the "catching up" of the church, which will occur at the beginning of the Tribulation that is coming upon the earth. . . . The second stage of Christ's coming will occur at the end of the Tribulation.[12]

During the tribulation, Jews will again have opportunity to turn to the Messiah and claim his eternal promises to them. So the rapture is the most significant event that introduces this time period in which the prophetic stopwatch relating to Israel's salvation begins ticking again. This interpretation allows for the final seven years of Daniel's prophecy to be fulfilled prior to Christ's establishment of his eternal kingdom.

Any current events that seem to lead up to this Jewish opportunity to claim God's promises in the tribulation excite Dispensationalists. They perceive recent history and present news stories relating to Israel to be indicators that God is culminating his mission on earth according to the prophecies made to Jews in the Old Testament. The rebirth of Israel as a nation, the resurgence of nations opposing the Jews, the gathering of resources and plans for rebuilding the Jerusalem temple, the mustering of power by deceitful political or religious leaders who could be the antichrist—all can be overlaid on the words of Daniel 9 as possible fulfillments of God's promises to his chosen people. If these interpretations are accurate, then the rapture is near and the ancient promises to Israel will soon be reengaged.

Since this understanding of a secret rapture is so key to Dispensational expectations of what will trigger the main events of the end times, we must ask, What evidence is there in the Bible for this kind of rapture? Darby grounded his ideas in 1 Thessalonians 4, where Paul tells his readers, "For the Lord himself will descend from heaven with a cry of command, with the voice of an archangel, and with the sound of the trumpet of God. And the dead in Christ will rise first. Then we who are alive, who are left, will be caught up together with them in the clouds to meet the Lord in the air, and so we will always be with the Lord" (vv. 16–17).

Prior to Darby, most Christians around the world interpreted this passage as describing events that will occur at Christ's final coming, prior to the judgment. Probably most Christians still think this, since the apostle's focus is on the *eternal* reunion that those who are still alive at Christ's return will experience with loved ones who have already gone to be with the Lord (notice v. 17 concludes with "and so we will *always* be with the Lord"). Nothing in the passage itself requires us to place it in a different time frame than that of Christ's final return to earth. However, Darby's view gained traction for two reasons. First, it helped explain other difficult Bible passages like Daniel 9. Second, it seemed to give Christians a way to understand deeply disappointing and difficult current events without losing hope. These events could be seen as precursors to God's final blessings and nearness to a raptured removal from earth's cruelties and corruptions.

Darby's view certainly offered a clear explanation for the final week of Daniel 9. His understanding of the secret rapture seemed also to fit with an important teaching of Jesus in Matthew 24: "Then two men will be in the field; one will be taken and one left. Two women will be grinding at the mill; one will be taken and one left. Therefore, stay awake, for you do not know on what day your Lord is coming" (vv. 40–42). This is where so many of the more imaginative descriptions of the secret rapture find their origin. If you have been exposed to a lot of *Left Behind* images and stories, Jesus's words seem to fit perfectly with the warnings about saints snatched from 747s with sinners left behind.

Yet, other Christians have seen the context of the Matthew 24 passage quite differently. They note that Jesus is cautioning about being unprepared for his second coming by referencing what happened to those who didn't heed warnings of the flood in the days of Noah. In the Genesis narrative, it's the saints who are left after the sinners are swept away by the desolations of the flood.

I don't intend to argue for which view is correct, only to help us understand why Darby's views have become so popular in our time. His views gained acceptance because they not only gave plausible explanations for difficult passages but also provided a way to make sense of difficult events in our present world.

The Scofield Effect

As mentioned earlier, Darby got a considerable boost in American evangelical churches (and in countries affected by their missionary efforts) when his views were featured in the notes of the Scofield Reference Bible. When the Scofield Bible was originally published in 1909 and revised by the author in 1917, it provided an immensely important and helpful resource for Bible-believing Christians. In those days the battle for the Bible was just getting into high gear. Higher critical scholarship from Europe was questioning the truth of Scripture, pitting science against God's

Word, and infecting many pulpits and denominations with sophisticated skepticism.

Against this onslaught of unbelief, Scofield offered a Bible with explanatory notes that ordinary Christians could understand from godly experts who trusted the Bible. For the first time since the publication of the Geneva Bible in 1560, ordinary people had ready access to commentary notes from Bible-believing scholars side-by-side with the biblical text. This made ordinary people in the pew competent readers of Scripture when so much of what paraded as scholarship was casting doubt on the Bible.

Scofield's notes included dates for biblical events that countered so-called scientific discoveries, interpretations that gave reasonable answers to new evolutionary theories of the creation of the cosmos and human origins, explanations for difficult texts that didn't disparage the Bible, and most especially, assurances of God's hand on the events of a world that was facing wars and epidemics of unprecedented horror. These multiple cataclysms that could destroy faith were countered with Scofield's clear explanations of how all was unfolding according to God's plan, within his sovereign control, and for the blessing of the people he would rescue from earth for eternity.

For the assurances people of faith needed, Scofield found Darby's ideas to be ideal. Difficult texts like Daniel 9, Matthew 24, and many portions of Revelation had accessible explanations. Also, in contrast to sophisticated claims that science and human goodness would soon rescue the world from evil, Darby's projections about the undoing of the world made sense in the face of wars, disasters, and disease—but with a profound hope still beaconing through. People were able to overlay the teachings of Scripture on the distressing events of the world and believe that they not only were witness to God's truth unfolding in real time but also were soon to see Christ's coming.

Such expectations only became more intense as the twentieth century unfolded with world wars, the flu pandemic of 1918, natural disasters, the Cold War, and Middle Eastern conflicts that seemed to put us on the doorstep of our final destiny. The result was a publishing phenomenon. The Scofield Reference Bible sold millions of copies and spawned incredibly popular books, conferences, movies, and ministries that helped to convince many Christians that Dispensational views were synonymous with Bible-believing Christianity—and that those who didn't have Dispensational views didn't really believe the Bible.

As we will see in the upcoming chapter, solid Dispensationalists have now modified their understanding of some of Darby's original views. Still, we need the background of this chapter to explain his significant contributions and influence. Dispensationalism gave many Christians a solid basis for trusting Scripture in the face of the twentieth century's theological and scientific skepticism, and it provided a basis for hope in the face of world events that threatened faith in a sovereign God. We shouldn't forget these blessings as we next consider specific aspects of Dispensationalism that set it apart from other end-times perspectives—and can also contribute to identifying the future hope all Christians share.

Dispensationalism Today

*T**he Late Great Planet Earth** by Hal Lindsey became the bestselling nonfiction book of the 1970s and eventually sold over thirty-five million copies. The book led to intense interest in Dispensational views of the end times and to the genuine conversion of many thousands to faith in Christ. The ability of Lindsey to fit the intrigue of the Cold War and the turmoil of the Middle East into end-times scenarios that he saw in the Bible was incredibly compelling. At a time of uncertainty, drug abuse, war, and moral decline, many hearts turned from hopelessness to preparedness for Jesus's return because of Lindsey's writings. He masterfully adapted Darby's Dispensationalism into highly accessible lessons for modern readers that had a profound blessing upon many individuals, churches, and schools.

Rebirth of the Nation of Israel

Lindsey stressed the prophetic significance of the rebirth of Israel: "The most important sign in Matthew has to be the restoration of the Jews to the land in the rebirth of Israel. . . . When the Jewish people, after nearly 2,000 years of exile, under relentless persecution, became a nation again on 14 May 1948 the 'fig tree' [a historic symbol of national Israel] put forth its first leaves."[1]

Many Christians today are unaware of how significant and difficult has been Israel's return to the land that God promised their forefathers. Not only were the Jews repeatedly exiled from their land during the Old Testament, but they have continued to fight for it their entire existence. During the Roman occupation, the Jewish people fought back three different times to reclaim control of their land. The first Jewish-Roman war (also known as the Great Revolt), was waged by the Roman general Titus in AD 66–73. He laid siege to Jerusalem and eventually destroyed both the city and the temple.

The second Jewish-Roman war, referred to as the Kitos War (AD 115–117), was conducted by a Roman general named Lucius Quietus. That conflict resulted in the slaughter of many Jewish people and caused further displacement from their homeland.

The final conflict between Israel and the Romans was initiated in AD 132 by the Jewish leader Simon bar Kochba. For three years the revolt was successful until Rome crushed the rebellion. According to the *World History Encyclopedia*, "Thousands of people were slaughtered and others scattered. Hadrian exiled all Jews from the region and prohibited their return on pain of death. Following the destruction of Judea and the resulting diaspora, Israel ceased to exist until the creation of the modern State of Israel in 1947–1948 CE by the United Nations."[2]

Lindsey explains his understanding of the significance of the twentieth century reestablishment of the Jewish nation this way:

> Jesus said that this would indicate that He was "at the door," ready to return. Then He said, "Truly I say to you, this generation will not pass away until all these things take place" (Matthew 24:34 NASB). What generation? Obviously, in context, the generation that would see the signs—chief among them the rebirth of Israel.

A generation in the Bible is something like forty years. If this is a correct deduction, then within forty years or so of 1948 [around 1988], all these things could take place.[3]

Lindsey later predicted that "the decade of the 1980s could very well be the last decade of history as we know it."[4] Many of his readers waited in anticipation for the rapture to occur as he had predicted, but obviously they were disappointed. What had Lindsey and other students of prophecy misunderstood about the rebirth of Israel?

Dr. David Jeremiah believes he has the answer. In his book *Is This the End?* he examines Ezekiel's prophecy about the "dry bones" of Israel:

> As I prophesied, there was a sound, and behold, a rattling, and the bones came together, bone to its bone. And I looked, and behold, there were sinews on them, and flesh had come upon them, and skin had covered them. But there was no breath in them. (Ezek. 37:7–8)

According to Dr. Jeremiah, "Just as these scattered, dry bones reassembled into their original human forms, the Jews who had been scattered all over the world would be reassembled in their original land. Yet the re-gathered nation would have no breath. It would be without spiritual life."[5]

He goes on to explain that this is the current state of Israel, but not its permanent condition according to Ezekiel.

> "Prophesy to the breath; prophesy, son of man, and say to the breath, Thus says the Lord GOD: Come from the four winds, O breath, and breathe on these slain, that they may live." So I prophesied as he commanded me, and the breath came into them, and they lived and stood on their feet, an exceedingly great army. (vv. 9–10)

Dr. Jeremiah asserts, "Here Ezekiel told us that God will, in time, put breath into the reassembled corpse of Israel. Obviously, this has not yet happened. But we can be assured that it will happen, just as God promised."[6]

The Tribulation and Second Coming

Though some Dispensational expectations have been modified in the light of modern events, others remain consistent among its classic advocates. Those who have been reared on Dispensational views will resonate with this summary of the seven-year tribulation given by Dr. John Walvoord, former president of Dallas Theological Seminary:

> Immediately after the rapture . . . a ten-nation group will form a political alliance in the Middle East. A leader will emerge who will gain control first of three and then of all ten (Dan. 7:8, 24–25). From this position of power, he will be able to enter into a covenant with Israel, bringing to rest the contentious relationship of Israel to its neighbors (9:27) and beginning the final seven-year countdown culminating in the second coming.[7]

The identities of the nations are not specified, but perspectives that have been shaped by recent events in our world make many church people think the ten nations will be some combination of Middle Eastern nations and Russia or China or some other superpower or rogue nation less obvious at this moment in history. Dispensationalists are usually less certain about the identity of the world leader the Bible calls the antichrist (1 John 2:18), but not about his activities during the tribulation. They believe that he will initially deceive the world into thinking he is a messianic leader. They cite the apostle Paul, who tells us, "The coming of the lawless one is by the activity of Satan with all power and false signs and wonders, and with all wicked deception for those who are perishing, because they refused to love the truth and so be saved" (2 Thess. 2:9–10).

Most Dispensationalists also believe that in the second half of the tribulation the antichrist's true nature will be revealed: "He will oppose and will exalt himself over everything that is called God or is worshiped, so that he sets himself up in God's temple, proclaiming himself to be God" (2 Thess. 2:4 NIV). Thus, as French Christians believed Robespierre revealed his evil by his abomination in Notre Dame Cathedral (see chap. 2), Dispensationalists believe the antichrist's arrogance will ultimately reveal the falseness of the religiosity that he has used to deceive many. He will change his claim from being a messianic leader to actually being God.

Dispensationalists also teach that during the tribulation the various judgments described in the book of Revelation (seals, trumpets, and bowls) will be poured out on humanity as an expression of God's wrath. "The Bible describes this as a time of 'war and slaughter everywhere' (Revelation 6:3–4). Widespread famine follows this global war (Revelation 6:5–6) and one-fourth of humanity dies (Revelation 6:7–8). . . . The remaining seal judgments bring more suffering and terrible events. These include the widespread martyrdom of Christians (Revelation 6:9–11)."[8]

The tribulation itself has significant stages in Dispensational thought. In a verse that is difficult to understand, the prophet Daniel says that "for half of the week [i.e., half of the seven-year period of the tribulation] he [i.e., the Antichrist] shall put an end to sacrifice and offering [in Israel]. And on the wing [i.e., temple section] of abominations shall come one who makes desolate, until the decreed end is poured out on the desolator" (Dan. 9:27). Most Dispensationalists interpret this to mean not only that the temple will be rebuilt in Jerusalem with a renewal of Old Testament sacrifices but also that the antichrist will ultimately turn from his benign dealings with Israel to defile the temple, stop the sacrifices, and persecute the people of God until he is destroyed as God has decreed.

God's decreed end of the antichrist will culminate in the battle of Armageddon. This will be the greatest showdown between good and evil in human history. Before the battle, Jesus will return. He will descend upon the Mount of Olives east of Jerusalem, splitting it in two (Zech. 14:3–4). He will then overthrow the antichrist "with the breath of his mouth" and destroy him "by the appearance [splendor] of his coming" (2 Thess. 2:8) that will include military engagement with the heavenly hosts in Christ's army (Rev. 19:11–16).

The Millennial Kingdom

According to most Dispensationalists, Christ's victory at Armageddon ushers in another important era: a literal, thousand-year reign of Christ on the earth that fulfills the Old Testament prophecies of his idyllic reign for Israel (Pss. 2; 72; Isa. 11; 65; Hab. 2).[9] In this scenario, Christ's final return to earth will occur before his millennial kingdom begins, but only after a period of tribulation from which the church has been rescued by the rapture that occurred with Christ's first return (see figure 4.1).

How do Dispensationalists arrive at this conclusion? Author Ron Rhodes explains that "in the chronology of the book of Revelation, the millennial kingdom clearly follows the second coming of Jesus Christ. Revelation 19 and 20 are chronological, with the second coming described in chapter 19 and the millennial kingdom described in chapter 20. The second coming lays a foundation for the establishment of the millennial kingdom."[10]

It's important that we understand what Dispensationalists believe about the millennium since, as we've already discussed in chapter 3, all major views about the end times base their distinctions on the timing and activity of Christ relative to this period. Dispensationalists believe Revelation teaches that Jesus will reign over all nations on the earth and Satan will be bound during the millennium "so that he might not deceive the nations any longer, until the thousand years were ended" (Rev. 20:1–3).

John Walvoord gives this description of what Christ's kingdom will be like during this time:

All kings bow down before Christ, and His rule extends from sea to sea. The earth will be filled with the glory of God. The desire of nations for peace, righteousness, knowledge of the Lord, economic justice, and deliverance from Satan will have its prophetic fulfillment. The major factors of the Millennium, including Christ's absolute power, will include the perfect and righteous government and ideal circumstances on the earth. In many respects, the rule of Christ as the last Adam replaces what God had intended for Adam, who was placed in charge of the garden of Eden.[11]

Who will be in the millennial kingdom? Dispensationalists believe the first group will be those who were raptured prior to the tribulation, which will include both Old and New Testament saints who died before the rapture, as well as those believers who were alive and caught up to meet Jesus in the air. This entire group will have immortal resurrection bodies and will reign with Christ on earth.[12]

The second group will include both Jewish and gentile believers who were alive at the second coming of Christ and who converted during the tribulation. They will remain in their mortal bodies, although Dispensationalists tell us that, according to Isaiah, they will have greater longevity: "No more shall there be in it an infant who lives but a few days, or an old man who does not fill out his days, for the young man shall die a hundred years old, and the sinner a hundred years old shall be accursed" (Isa. 65:20).

As mentioned previously, Satan will be released at the end of the millennium and will lead a brief revolt ("Satan's little season") against Christ and his followers (see figure 4.1). However, he will be swiftly defeated and thrown into the lake of fire (Rev. 20:7–10). Then all unbelievers throughout history will be resurrected and judged at the great white throne of judgment (20:11–15). They will be found guilty and cast into the lake of fire, along with death and Hades. Believers who died during the millennium will also be raised from the dead and will live forever with Christ in resurrected bodies.

Where Will Believers Spend Eternity?

Many early Dispensationalists believed that the church would spend eternity in heaven while Israel would spend eternity on a renewed earth. Some still affirm this view, as indicated in the article "Where Will We Spend Eternity? Heaven or Earth?":

> God's purpose in and through the Nation of Israel is the earth and placing His Kingdom *on the earth*. That is clear even from the prayer the Lord Jesus taught in Matthew 6:10. On the other hand, God's purpose for the Body of Christ (who we are) involves reconciling the heavens back to his authority. The purpose of the Body of Christ according [to] Paul's epistles is *for the heavens*. II Corinthians 5:1 says our house and new home is "*eternal in the heavens.*" I Thessalonians 4:13–18 says when the rapture occurs and we meet the Lord in the air—"so shall we ever be with the Lord." *We are with Him in the heavens*.[13]

This perspective is consistent with Dispensational assumptions that God has a different plan for Israel and the church and that the eternal promises he made to his chosen people about the land of Israel will be honored (see Gen. 17:8).

However, today not all Dispensationalists agree with that early view. As more and more Bible-believing, Dispensational scholars seek to teach only what they can prove from specific New Testament texts, it seems increasingly unlikely to them that God intends to maintain separate communities of believers in heaven and on earth. The new Jerusalem comes from heaven, is entered by people from every nation, and has all the blessings of heaven that every believer will enjoy in eternity, including the eternal presence of Jesus (Rev. 21:2–4, 24–26).

Craig Blaising, former executive vice president and provost of Southwestern Baptist Theological Seminary, writes of how such biblical descriptions have affected Dispensational views: "Beginning in the late 1950s, some dispensationalists began to abandon classical dispensationalism's dualism of heavenly and earthly eternal states."[14] This meant that all Dispensationalists needed to choose between a perspective that kept Israel living forever in an earthly reality or ultimately living with the church in a heavenly existence.

Pastor John MacArthur still favors the earthly viewpoint, but he also provides an explanation reconciling the earlier and later views by picturing all nations in one eternal reality. He writes that "in the consummation of all things, God will renovate the heavens and the earth, merging His heaven with a new universe for a perfect dwelling-place that will be our home forever. In other words, heaven, the realm where God dwells, will expand to encompass the entire universe of creation, which will be fashioned into a perfect and glorious domain fit for the glory of heaven."[15]

Progressive Dispensationalism

These small shifts in Dispensational thought that allow for some merging of God's eternal plan for Israel and the church are the result of conscientious Christian leaders' commitment to keep examining Scripture to confirm their understanding of the end times. That faithful commitment to let God's Word have the final word has resulted in other shifts that we need to understand to honor our ultimate goal of seeing what unites all Christians in their end-times hope.

In the late 1970s and early 1980s two Dallas Theological Seminary graduates, Darrell Bock and Craig Blaising, began their doctoral studies at the University of Aberdeen. Dallas Seminary was a historic bastion of Dispensational thought, and both men had been fully instructed in classic Dispensational Premillennialism.

However, through their conscientious study of the Bible, they became convinced that certain aspects of traditional Dispensationalism could not be biblically sustained. Their commitment to Scripture was so unassailable that, after they completed their doctoral work, both became professors at Dallas Seminary where their biblical studies deepened.

Bock and Blaising began to meet with other scholars committed to Scripture to refine certain aspects of traditional Dispensationalism according to their biblical understanding. In the early 1990s three key books were published to explain how traditional Dispensationalism could progress to conform more closely with what these men believed could be proven from Scripture. The first two were written by Bock and Blaising: *Dispensationalism, Israel and the Church* and *Progressive Dispensationalism*. The third book, *The Case for Progressive Dispensationalism*, was written by Robert Saucy.[16]

These works make it obvious that much of what is now identified as the Progressive Dispensational view of the last days is almost identical to the traditional Dispensationalist view. Most Progressives still believe in a pretribulation rapture of the church, a literal seven-year tribulation, the global rule of the antichrist during the tribulation, and a literal, thousand-year millennial kingdom on earth after Christ returns. They also believe God will fulfill his promises to Israel during the millennium. This is important to note for traditional Dispensationalists who may worry that revisions to the classic system are tantamount to a rejection of its most notable features.

So how do Progressive Dispensational views differ from traditional Dispensationalism? Although Charles Ryrie did not identify as a Progressive Dispensationalist, he provides a helpful summary of what Progressives believe about a number of topics:

1. *The Literal Interpretation of Scripture.* "A complementary hermeneutic must be used alongside a literal hermeneutic.

This means that the New Testament makes complementary changes to Old Testament promises without jettisoning those original promises."

2. *The Unifying Theme of Scripture.* "The kingdom of God is the unifying theme of biblical history."

3. *Israel and the Church.* "The concept of the church as completely distinct from Israel and as a mystery unrevealed in the Old Testament needs revising, making the idea of two purposes and two peoples of God invalid."

4. *The Davidic Covenant.* "Christ has already inaugurated the Davidic reign in heaven at the right hand of the Father, which equals the throne of David, though He does not yet reign as Davidic king on earth during the Millennium."

5. *The Number of Dispensations.* "Within biblical history there are four dispensational eras."

6. *The New Covenant.* "The new covenant has already been inaugurated, though its blessings are not yet fully realized until the Millennium."

7. *Holistic Redemption.* "The one divine plan of holistic redemption encompasses all people and all areas of human life—personal, societal, cultural, and political."[17]

From this it becomes apparent how a number of key ideas that distinguish traditional Dispensationalism have now been put in question by the Progressives' biblical scruples. Let's consider several of these in more depth.

The Literal Interpretation of Scripture

As mentioned in chapter 4, traditional Dispensationalists claim that they alone use the literal approach to Bible interpretation *consistently.* They think all others, including Progressive Dispensationalists, revert to spiritualizing biblical texts to support their views. However, Craig Blaising disagrees. He says, "It should be noted that progressive dispensationalism is not an abandonment of 'literal' interpretation for 'spiritual' interpretation. Progressive dispensationalism is a development of 'literal' interpretation into a more consistent historical-literary interpretation."[18]

What does that mean? Blaising and Bock claim that since all conservative Christians acknowledge that God's revelation is progressive (no pun intended), in that God's redemptive message becomes clearer as we progress through the Bible, then we can expect Old Testament revelation to become clearer and more specific over time. In their words, "Old Testament promise has not been replaced; it has been opened up, clarified, expanded, and periodized in the progress of apostolic reflection on Jesus' teaching and actions."[19] The meaning of Old Testament promises hasn't been spiritualized or turned into symbols by identifying aspects of their fulfillment in the church. Rather, the promises are seen according to their fully intended meaning that has been made clearer by the progress of biblical history.

For example, God promised Abraham that his descendants would become as numerous as the stars in the heavens and that all the nations of the earth would be blessed in him (Gen. 22:15–18). That original promise certainly included both the future nation of Israel and the gentile nations. Beyond that, its full meaning was vague. But by the time of the apostles and the establishment of the New Testament church, the promise became clearer and more specific. It was fulfilled through Jesus, the promised Messiah and the ultimate "seed" of Abraham (Gal. 3:16 NIV). Further, those gentiles who believe in Jesus are included in God's covenant with Abraham. The church isn't a replacement of the Abrahamic covenant but the expanded and intended fulfillment of it (Rom. 9:4–8; Gal. 3:7–9).

Israel and the Church

Although Progressive Dispensationalists still believe that Israel and the church are two separate entities, they refine the distinctions of these two groups. Bock and Blaising state, "The appearance of the church does not signal a secondary redemption plan, either to be fulfilled in heaven apart from the new earth or in an elite class of Jews and Gentiles who are forever distinguished from the rest of redeemed humanity. Instead, the church today is a revelation of spiritual blessings which all the redeemed will share in spite of their ethnic and national differences."[20]

In the Progressive Dispensationalist view, Israel's distinctions remain ethnic, national, and territorial. The true people of Israel are Jewish (ethnic). Many live in the nation of Israel (national). And just like any other nation, that nation has boundaries (territorial). God still has a plan for this nation; however, that plan doesn't require that he provide for their eternal destiny in a way different from any other people. After all, the church is made up of believers from *every* nation, including Israel.

This means that Jewish Christians can simultaneously be members of both the nation of Israel and the worldwide church. Therefore, there's no biblical reason for claiming that God cannot deal with both Israel and the church at the same time. That means the great parenthesis isn't necessary or biblical. There's no need to claim that the Old Testament prophets did not reference the church when it seems that in fact they did (cf. Gen. 17:5; Isa. 49:6; Luke 4:18–19; Acts 2:16). The ticking clock of biblical prophecy doesn't need to stop when ethnic Jews rejected Jesus and the church began. And as we shall soon see, neither is the rapture required to remove the church from the earth so that God may restart his program for Israel.

These are significant departures from traditional Dispensationalism, and those in its ranks know so. In his widely read and frequently updated book *Dispensationalism*, Charles Ryrie contends that maintaining the distinction of God's programs for Israel and the church is indispensable to the tenets of Dispensationalism:

> A dispensationalist keeps Israel and the church distinct. . . . Fuller says, "the basic premise of Dispensationalism is two purposes God

expressed in the formation of two peoples who maintain their distinction throughout eternity." . . . This is probably the most basic theological test of whether or not a person is a dispensationalist, and it is undoubtedly the most practical and conclusive. The one who fails to distinguish Israel and the church consistently will inevitably not hold to dispensational distinctions; and the one who does will.[21]

It's so important to note that some of those now identifying themselves as Dispensationalists no longer hold to this distinction on which the system was built.[22] I note this not to disparage the system but to celebrate the Lord's removal of a barrier between many Dispensationalists and other Bible-believing brothers and sisters. So much can be done to unite us all in our end-times hope when we aren't holding to distinctions the Bible doesn't clearly support. Other hopeful shifts are also occurring to move Dispensationalists and non-Dispensationalists together on the following subjects.

The Number of Dispensations

Progressive Dispensationalists tend to emphasize only four dispensations rather than the eight (or nine if eternity is included) illustrated in figure 3.1. These are:

- Patriarchal (from creation to Sinai)
- Mosaic (from Sinai to Messiah's ascension)
- Ecclesial (from the ascension to Messiah's second coming)
- Zionic (from Christ's return into eternity, which is subdivided into millennial and eternal eras)[23]

It should also be noted that "progressive dispensationalists, in addition to viewing the dispensations as chronologically successive, also view them as progressive stages in salvation history."[24] This understanding moves those holding Dispensational and Covenantal perspectives much closer together (cf. figures 3.1 and 3.2).[25]

Holistic Redemption

According to Progressive Dispensationalists, holistic redemption means that Christ's redemption of his world and people "covers personal, communal, social, political, and national aspects of human life."[26] Progressive Dispensationalists place a greater emphasis on social action, both inside and outside the church, than their traditional counterparts. Although Progressives teach that holistic redemption will only be completely fulfilled in the millennium, they still believe it should be part of the ministry of the church in every stage of history.

Because traditional Dispensationalism was birthed more as a reaction to and a promise of escape from societal ills and natural disasters, its focus has rarely been on ministries of mercy or creation care. As a shift occurs to more consideration of Christ's and the apostles' concern for redemption of the entire created order, including the poor, oppressed, and damaged (Matt. 25:40; James 1:27), Dispensationalism takes a step toward perspectives that see the end times or the millennium as the culmination of the church's caring influence on the whole world.

The Pretribulation Rapture

Although the timing of the rapture isn't mentioned in Ryrie's list of Progressive Dispensational distinctives, it's worth mentioning. No feature of Dispensationalism receives more attention in popular media, has more significance in many Christians' thoughts about the events of the last days, or has caused more division and derision among Christians of differing views. However, if those in Dispensational ranks now say that the great parenthesis isn't biblical and that God can deal simultaneously with the church and Israel, then a pretribulation rapture is no longer necessary. In addition, the details and sequence of other events of the last days that were determined by their relationship to the rapture can be held with less tenacity.

93

This doesn't mean that the rapture is untrue or that Progressive Dispensationalists don't affirm it. What it does mean is that a pretribulation rapture is apparently not as critical to biblical belief as traditional Dispensationalism once taught. After all, if God doesn't need to remove the church from the earth prior to restarting his program with Israel, then the secret rapture becomes far less essential to end-times expectations.

I need to emphasize that many Progressive Dispensationalists still believe in the pretribulation rapture. Robert L. Thomas, who teaches New Testament at The Master's Seminary, writes, "For the most part, progressive dispensationalists believe in a Rapture prior to the future seven-year tribulation, but they do so in a rather tentative fashion. Their system could dispense with this doctrine without altering their position significantly."[27]

Both Craig Blaising and Darrell Bock believe in the pretribulation rapture. Bock writes,

> The most important passage is probably from 1 Thessalonians 4:15 to the end, in which there's a discussion about meeting the Lord in the air and the next chapter discusses issues on antichrist, a part of tribulation period. If you take those two chapters in sequence, then the return of the Lord for believers would come before the antichrist experience and the second coming really is a coming to earth to deal with the evil that's associated with antichrist. (1 Thess. 5:1–10)[28]

The reason that the secret rapture stays in place isn't merely to keep peace in Dispensational ranks. As we will see, all major end-times views teach that a rapture will occur when Jesus returns to gather his people to himself. It's the idea of a *secret* rapture that has distinguished Dispensationalism. Why do Dispensationalists keep this distinction? They're being true to convictions that once shaped Dispensationalism and now hold promise to heal divisions and unite hearts among Bible-believing churches across the world. That's simply to say, they're trying to let Scripture rule their thoughts and attitudes.

Those who have advanced the Progressive Dispensational perspective have done so out of a conscientious commitment to continue teaching only what they believe they can demonstrate from Scripture. They have often done this at great cost, especially when questioning former aspects of the Dispensational system that were seemingly indispensable. As a result, Progressive Dispensational perspectives have gained much credibility among those most informed and committed to Scripture. Progressive perspectives are probably now embraced by the greatest number of Bible-believing professors at Dispensational schools, such as Dallas Seminary, Talbot Seminary, Moody Bible Institute, and Cornerstone Seminary (formerly Grand Rapids Theological Seminary).

Traditional Dispensationalism is probably still the most popular view among North American churchgoers and internet commentators. A century of association with biblical faithfulness in the face of unbelieving attacks on the truth of Scripture has anchored the classic distinctives into the thinking of God's people. However, if trusted scholars from Dispensationalism's own ranks have been rethinking aspects of the system that are as foundational as what is meant by "literal" interpretation, the distinction of the divine plans for Israel and the church, and the necessity of the secret rapture, then there is the opportunity for Christians across Dispensational, Covenantal, and denominational divides to consider what each has to offer about the hope we share in God's promises. That's a good reason to press on to consider the other views regarding the end times.

Historic Premillennial View, Part 1

People and Perspectives

H istoric and Dispensational Premillennialists have a lot in common. They both believe there will be a thousand-year reign of Christ on earth. They agree that Christ will return before that millennium—that's why they are both labeled as *pre*millennialists. Many agree that God's promises to the nation of Israel will one day be fulfilled. All agree that there will be a time of severe tribulation prior to the Lord's glorious return.

But despite their similarities, their differences are significant. Many Dispensational Premillennialists have become world-famous authors with books like the Left Behind series and *The Late Great Planet Earth*. Some of them are household names, such as Charles Ryrie, Tim LaHaye, and Dr. David Jeremiah.

Then there are the Historic Premillennialists. In some ways they remind me of a story a friend once told me. One day after church he went to lunch with some fellow churchgoers who had just read

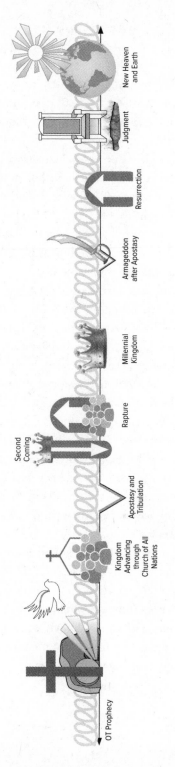

Figure 6.1
Historic Premillennial View of the End Times

OT Prophecy

Kingdom Advancing through Church of All Nations

Apostasy and Tribulation

Second Coming

Rapture

Millennial Kingdom

Armageddon after Apostasy

Resurrection

Judgment

New Heaven and Earth

Continuous fulfillment of prophetic prediction and Christ's kingdom purposes.

the Left Behind series. They were very excited about what they had learned and asked him what he thought of the series. He admitted that he hadn't read any of the books because he didn't share the authors' view of the last days. They looked at him in bewilderment and asked, "Is there another view?"

Many people today who are fascinated with the end times would be hard pressed to mention a single author, pastor, or TV personality who is a Historic Premillennialist. Try asking someone at your church if they have heard of George Eldon Ladd, R. Laird Harris, or J. Barton Payne. You'll probably get a blank stare. Those who hold the historic view are the forgotten siblings in the premillennial family. But that was not always the case.

Historic Premillennialists have at least one claim to fame. They are called "historic" because there's good evidence that most people in the early church held this view, including church fathers such as Irenaeus, Justin Martyr, and Papias.[1]

Robert G. Clouse, editor of the respected book *The Meaning of the Millennium*, says that this version of premillennialism appears to have been the dominant end-times view during the first three centuries of the Christian era.[2] Likewise, Arthur Skevington Wood (1916–1993) states that "it must be conceded that in the first three centuries the premillennial interpretation predominated."[3] When these authors say "premillennial," they mean Historic Premillennialism, not Dispensational Premillennialism, which they claim made its first appearance in the writings of John Nelson Darby in the mid-1800s.

In this chapter we'll explore distinguishing features of Historic Premillennialism, and this path will lead us to discover some of its differences from Dispensational Premillennialism. George Eldon Ladd offers this brief summary of Historic Premillennialism: "After the Second Coming of Christ, he will reign for a thousand years over the earth before the final consummation of God's redemptive purpose in the new heavens and the new earth. . . . This is the natural reading of Revelation 20:1–6."[4]

Since Ladd sees this as the most "natural" reading of Revelation 20:1–6, he interprets surrounding portions of Revelation so as to be consistent with this understanding. Revelation 19:11–16 shows how Christ's second coming as a conqueror over the antichrist, Satan, and death sets up the millennial reign of Jesus. Thus, the verses that follow give the sequence of these events. First, the Lord binds Satan (20:1) so that he can "deceive the nations no more" (20:3). Satan's restriction coincides with the "first resurrection" of believers who share in Christ's rule throughout the millennium (20:5). Then, after a thousand years, Satan is loosed and defeated in a final war that results in his being cast into the lake of fire. Satan's demise triggers a second resurrection of those who had not been raised prior to the millennium. They appear before the throne of God for final judgment, with the justified inheriting everlasting life and the unjust sent to everlasting punishment.

So, what exactly distinguishes this Historic Premillennial view, which says Christ will appear before the millennium, from the Dispensational Premillennial view, which also says Jesus will come before his thousand-year reign on earth? Both views are obviously premillennial.

Old Testament Prophecy

One of the main differences between Dispensational and Historic Premillennialists is the way they interpret Old Testament prophecies. George Eldon Ladd (1911–1982), who was one of the foremost modern advocates of Historic Premillennialism, identifies what he considers a key difference. He says that Dispensationalism bases its view of the end times on a literal interpretation of the Old Testament and then tries to make the New Testament fit into that perspective. By contrast, he says that his non-Dispensational perspective is based on the explicit teaching of the New Testament.[5]

In other words, Historic Premillennialists believe that the New Testament writers were inspired by the Holy Spirit to interpret Old

Testament prophecies in ways that more fully explain God's intention for the original texts than the original human writers or readers may have understood. This would mean that the New Testament authors themselves don't follow a Dispensational understanding of the literal reading of Old Testament prophecies. Rather, Historic Premillennialists think we need to interpret prophetic fulfillments according to the ways that New Testament authors, inspired by the Holy Spirit, explained how the grace of God unfolding before them was the fulfillment of God's original promises.[6]

Ladd provides a sample illustration of the way New Testament authors often read the Old Testament:

> Matthew 2:15 quotes from Hosea 11:1 to prove from Scripture that Jesus must come from Egypt. ["Out of Egypt I called my son."] This, however, is not what the prophecy means in the Old Testament. Hosea says, "When Israel was a child, I loved him, and out of Egypt I called my son." In Hosea this is not a prophecy at all but a historical affirmation that God had called Israel out of Egypt in the Exodus. However, Matthew recognizes Jesus to be God's greater son. . . . *The Old Testament is reinterpreted* in light of the Christ event.[7]

Contemporary Historic Premillennialists would add insights from the last three decades of Hebrew narrative studies. Such studies reveal that Matthew quoted Hosea to remind readers of God's consistent pattern of rescuing his people (actually referred to as God's "son" in Exod. 4:23) through events related to Egypt (the land that God used to rescue his people from famine, slavery, and enemies in multiple Old Testament accounts). Matthew isn't saying Hosea meant to prophesy Christ's childhood time in Egypt, but that people on this side of the cross can look back and understand how the pattern of events in Christ's life are consistent with the ancient prophet's observation of how God repeatedly provided for his people's rescue. Just as Egypt was often God's haven for developing the rescue of his people in the Old Testament, so it served New Testament people by providing a haven for their Redeemer until after the death of Herod.

The repetitive Old Testament events related to Egypt prepared God's people to understand who Christ was and how his ministry would unfold, as do many other patterns of Old Testament sacrifices, temple practices, kingdom features, and so forth. Historic Premillennialists would say that in a similar way, repeated Old Testament prophecies about God's extension of his grace to all people groups, who would eventually be identified as his beloved (Rom. 9:24–26), were preparing us for the ministry of the church (9:33; 15:8–12).

For example, the Old Testament priests and prophets didn't fully understand how the temple sacrifices would foreshadow and predict the ministry of Jesus, but the Holy Spirit did. So when the apostles read back into the Old Testament details of Christ's work, they are not being unfaithful to Old Testament meanings but are illuminating them more fully and according to their inspired intent. Similarly, although the church wasn't fully anticipated by the Old Testament prophets, their words, activities, and relationships revealed God's gracious provision for a kingdom expanding to all people and thus signaled the coming church. Historic Premillennialists aren't bothered by saying the signals are more clearly understood after the church appears; they simply believe this was the Holy Spirit's intention when he inspired the Old Testament writers who prophesied more than their immediate context allowed them to understand (cf. Acts 15:14–17; Rom. 15:8–12; 16:25–26; Eph. 3:5–6).

As we saw in previous chapters, because of their commitment to their version of literal interpretation, classical Dispensationalists don't believe that the Old Testament prophets foresaw the church age. Dispensationalists would insist that the Old Testament's prophetic promises given to Israel apply only to that nation. However, these same Dispensationalists would generally agree with Historic

Premillennialists that many Old Testament prophecies also spoke of future blessings for the gentiles. Historic Premillennialists (and Progressive Dispensationalists) see such passages as necessarily indicating God's plans for the coming of the church, not because the Old Testament prophets understood the full meaning of what they were saying but because inspired New Testament writers explain and apply the fullness to us.[8]

Historic Premillennialists recognize that the human author of a biblical text was not its only author. No Scripture was simply a product of human insight or invention. Rather, holy men of God spoke as they were carried along by the Holy Spirit, who wouldn't have had the limitations of human perspective or purpose (2 Pet. 1:20–21). Consider, for example, how the apostle Paul uses the Old Testament prophecies to urge others to accept God's expanding work in the church: "The Scripture, foreseeing that God would justify the Gentiles by faith, preached the gospel beforehand to Abraham, saying, 'In you shall all the nations be blessed.' So then, those who are of faith are blessed along with Abraham, the man of faith" (Gal. 3:8–9).

Paul doesn't say Moses understood that the church was being prophesied by these words about Abraham but that "Scripture" foresaw "that God would justify the Gentiles by faith." Scripture, inspired by the Holy Spirit, anticipated the expanding blessings of the church. We can multiply the number of passages where the New Testament writers similarly urged readers to interpret the Old Testament in terms of God's plans for the church (e.g., Acts 2:16–17; 13:46–47; Rom. 10:11–21). When Old Testament passages that unquestionably reflect God's intention to spread his grace beyond the people of Israel are read through the gospel lens of the New Testament writers, then God's plans for the church seem emblazoned throughout Scripture.

The apostle Peter urged Jewish acceptance of the church's ministry to the gentiles because "all the prophets bear witness that everyone who believes in him [Jesus] receives forgiveness of sins through his name" (Acts 10:43). Consider how Peter would have understood the following Old Testament passages:

Genesis 12:2–3: "I will make of you a great nation, and I will bless you and make your name great, so that you will be a blessing. I will bless those who bless you, and him who dishonors you I will curse, and in you all the families of the earth shall be blessed." This prophetic promise we identify as the Abrahamic Covenant by which God initiated and enabled his provision for many people outside Israel to experience his grace by the faith of Abraham (Gal. 3:8). So critical is this covenant to our understanding of God's gracious mission for the world that he explains and reiterates it numerous times, even in the opening book of the Bible where it was first recorded (Gen. 15:5–6; 17:4–5; 18:18; 22:18).

Psalm 22:27: "All the ends of the earth shall remember and turn to the Lord, and all the families of the nations shall worship before you."

Psalm 86:9: "All the nations you have made shall come and worship before you, O Lord, and shall glorify your name."

Isaiah 49:6: Speaking to Israel, the Lord said, "I will make you as a light for the nations, that my salvation may reach to the end of the earth."

Daniel 7:14: Here, the prophet sees a vision of "a son of man"—a title Jesus applied to himself—approaching the Ancient of Days. Then Daniel prophetically observes that the son of man "was given dominion and glory and a kingdom, that all peoples, nations, and languages should serve him."

Malachi 1:11: In the final book of the Old Testament, the Lord proclaims, "'My name will be great among the nations, and in every place incense will be offered to my name, and a pure offering. For my name will be great among the nations,' says the Lord of hosts."

The Church and Israel

Because they perceive God's plan for extending his grace as unfolding across Scripture, Historic Premillennialists don't believe God has two separate and nonoverlapping programs for Israel and the church.[9] Unlike traditional Dispensationalists, who believe that Israel's prophetic stopwatch ceased ticking when the church age began, Historic Premillennialists would prefer to think of prophecy as an atomic clock that never ceases to tick!

An Atomic Clock Perspective

Historic Premillennialists say that God has never deviated from his original plan. He has had a determined purpose since the beginning of the world—to *display* his glory in the grace that's first claimed by faith through Israel and then to *expand* the provision of that grace to all who will receive his redemption (Acts 15:15–17; Rom. 1:16). Old Testament saints weren't fully prepared to receive God's plan for the nations (e.g., Jon. 3:10–4:4). And their prophets didn't fully understand the dimensions of the gospel (1 Pet. 1:10–12), but the Holy Spirit inspired them to reveal it in ways that gave proof and foundation to the ministry and mission of the church in the fullness of God's timing. This is why Peter, a Jewish apostle, would preach, "We believe that we will be saved through the grace of the Lord Jesus, just as they [i.e., gentiles] will" (Acts 15:11). Salvation was being provided to Jews and gentiles by the same plan of grace.

So how do Historic Premillennialists view the relationship between Israel and the church? They point to the apostle Paul's explanation of God's plan to extend his grace to Jewish and gentile believers in the church. Rather than telling Jews that they have been totally rejected, Paul tells gentile believers at Rome that they have been enfolded into God's plan for his chosen people (Rom. 11:19–24).

The apostle compares Israel to a damaged olive tree into which new branches of humanity have been grafted. Paul then addresses new gentile converts this way: "But if some of the branches [of the original olive tree] were broken off, and you, although a wild olive shoot, were grafted in among the others and now share in the nourishing root of the olive tree, do not be arrogant toward the branches. If you are, remember it is not you who support the root, but the root that supports you" (Rom. 11:17–18). The olive tree still lives; its roots support life old and new.

Jewish believers would understand the context of these words. In the Old Testament, God refers to Israel as an olive tree: "The LORD once called you 'a green olive tree, beautiful with good fruit'" (Jer. 11:16). If gentiles are grafted into this historic olive tree, then God's plan for Israel continues. Historic Premillennialists don't believe that in the New Testament God replaced his original olive tree with another tree of faith. Instead, gentile believers (wild olive shoots) have been grafted into Israel and share in the benefits of God's covenant with Abraham and his descendants. These new branches aren't superior to the tree into which they have been grafted, but neither are they separate. Now both Jews and gentiles are God's people, unified in the life of grace that comes from the same nourishing root of God's provision.

Paul reiterates this in his letter to the church in Galatia, reflecting on God's ancient covenant promise to Abraham: "Through your offspring all nations on earth will be blessed." Paul knows that in Hebrew the word translated as "offspring" can also mean "seed" (i.e., descendant). Abraham's ultimate "seed" is Jesus Christ himself, through whom all God's promises for the nations are fulfilled. Therefore, Paul concludes that "if you belong to Christ, then you are Abraham's seed, and heirs according to the promise" (Gal. 3:29 NIV). Because Jesus is Abraham's seed, all who are united to Christ by faith—both Jews and gentiles—are spiritual descendants of Abraham. Gentiles are adopted (engrafted) into the Jewish family according to God's covenant promise and eternal plan.

From a Historic Premillennial perspective, all Christians are Jews by spiritual adoption. Jews aren't discarded in favor of gentile believers, and Israel isn't replaced by the church (Rom. 11:28–32). Every believer in the church is a spiritual member of the family of Abraham, who was distinguished by his faith in God's promised provision. That may be a new thought to you. Yet it's precisely what the apostle Paul teaches: "If you are Christ's, then you are Abraham's offspring" (Gal. 3:29; see also 3:7–9).

This perspective should discredit every speck of prejudice and hatred that Jewish people have received from Christians throughout the centuries. Excusing bigotry by saying "Jews killed Jesus" ignores the spiritual reality that it was human sin—mine and yours—that nailed Jesus to the cross (1 Cor. 15:3; 1 Pet. 2:24). Beyond that, if we're united to Christ by faith, then we're engrafted into his Jewish heritage (Gal. 3:6–7). All true Christians are Jews—not by birth but by faith in the covenant promises originally made to Abraham. We're Jews by faith if we have trusted in the Jewish Carpenter to be our Savior.

As we consider this relationship of Israel and the church from the perspective of Historic Premillennialists, we need to underscore an important similarity with Dispensationalists. The fact that gentiles have been grafted into the faith that was made available through Israel doesn't mean that God has abandoned his plans for his chosen people. Paul says that the original "root" nourishes all believers. God still has plans for this root (Rom. 11:2, 5).

Just as many Dispensationalists believe that God still has future plans for those rooted in Abraham, so do many Historic Premillennialists.[10] They believe this because of statements the apostle Paul made to new gentile believers:

> Lest you be wise in your own sight, I do not want you to be unaware of this mystery, brothers: a partial hardening has come upon Israel, until the fullness of the Gentiles has come in. And in this way all Israel will be saved, as it is written,

"The Deliverer will come from Zion,
  he will banish ungodliness from Jacob";
"and this will be my covenant with them
  when I take away their sins."

As regards the gospel, they are enemies for your sake. But as regards election, they are beloved for the sake of their forefathers. For the gifts and the calling of God are irrevocable. (Rom. 11:25–29)

Paul could have said that since Jews had largely rejected Jesus, God would totally reject them. But that is not Paul's point. He says that only a "partial hardening" to the gospel of Jesus Christ has come upon those who are Jews by birth. Not all will be rejected. Why? Paul says this is because "they are beloved for the sake of their forefathers." The "gifts and the calling of God [made known through Abraham] are irrevocable."

Such words convince many Historic Premillennialists that God intends for many ethnic Jews to realize that Jesus is truly their Messiah. They will place their faith in Jesus, the Lord will take away their sins, and they will receive the blessings of Messiah originally promised to their forefathers. Such Jews will be the children of Abraham by birth and by faith. In this way God's promises to Israel are maintained for ethnic Jews, even as those promises are extended to people of all nations by their adoption into the family of Abraham on the basis of their faith (Gal. 3:9).

Paul is careful to say that God's covenant blessings fall only upon those whose faith is genuine (Rom. 2:28–29). He doesn't promise covenant blessings to those who are only physically descended from Abraham, those who are only ethnically or nationally identified with Israel. To the contrary, he says that "not all who are descended from Israel belong to Israel" (9:6). Physical descent isn't sufficient for covenant inclusion. "It is not the children of the flesh who are the children of God, but the children of the promise are counted as [Abraham's] offspring" (9:8). What was the promise? God's promise to bless those who, like Abraham, place their faith in his gracious provision.

There were Old Testament Jews by birth who didn't receive God's blessings because they rejected his grace (see 1 Cor. 10:1–5). However, covenant blessings that were promised to Abraham for all who put their faith in God's provision always did, and always do, apply to all those who trust in God's grace rather than their own accomplishments or righteousness (Rom. 9:30–32). Because some of those who rightly believe are also Jewish by birth, God's covenant plan is shown to be irrevocable. His love for Jews remains intact. "They are beloved for the sake of their forefathers" (11:28), so a "remnant of them will be saved" along with people from all nations who put their faith in Jesus (9:25–27).

There are important reasons to underscore the apostle Paul's distinction between those who are merely Jews by birth and those who are children of Abraham by birth and belief. One is that sometimes North American Christians forget to distinguish between Jews who are born again and those who are Jews by ethnicity—between spiritually alive Jews and Jews who merely live in Israel. While our love for Jewish people must continue to motivate our care for their souls, we must be careful not to confuse compassion for our Jewish brothers and sisters with unexamined support of all the policies and practices of those who are Jews by birth living in the nation of Israel. All nations err, and we must not forget the biblical demands of justice and mercy, even as we support the security concerns of people we love.

Key to the thought of Historic Premillennialists is the perspective that there is only one people of God: those who are united to Christ by faith in his provision. This also means there is only one plan of salvation: we are saved by grace alone through faith alone in Christ alone. There is no human era in which God's grace has not been made known. His grace is necessary for the rescue of our souls from personal sin and the corruptions of our first parents. From the moment God declared to Satan that he would provide a Redeemer to rescue fallen humanity (Gen. 3:15), two truths became clear: (1) the Redeemer would come; and (2) you are not your Redeemer. There are no exceptions. There never have been. Those who will live eternally with God are those who have entirely placed their hope in his Son.

Historic Premillennial View, Part 2

Events

The Rapture

Historic Premillennialists believe in a rapture (see figure 6.1).[1] However, they do not believe there will be a *secret* rapture of the church with a second coming of Christ prior to the tribulation that is then followed by *another* second coming of Christ prior to the millennium (cf. figure 4.1). Historic Premillennialists contend that the Bible never speaks of two second comings of Christ. Instead, they believe the plainest reading of the Bible is that Jesus will "snatch up" or "catch up" his people in the air to accompany his second and final return to earth in power and great glory. This rapture is not secret but rather is the glorious announcement and preparation for the millennial kingdom in which Christ's people will reign with him for a thousand years upon the earth.

A secret rapture for non-Jews is only necessary for traditional Dispensationalists because of their belief that God must remove the church from the earth so that the prophetic stopwatch relating to Israel can begin ticking again. Since Historic Premillennialists believe the church is engrafted into Israel, they see no problem with God working with all his people at the same time. There's no need to extricate gentile believers if Jesus is about to establish his millennial kingdom for everyone on earth. Historic Premillennialists believe that the rapture is real but not secret.

But doesn't the Bible describe the nature of the secret rapture when Paul writes, "We who are alive . . . will be caught up together . . . in the clouds to meet the Lord in the air" (1 Thess. 4:17)? This definitely describes the rapture, but there's nothing in this text to characterize it as secret or indicate that these events occur at a time separate from Christ's final, glorious return. Historic Premillennialists say that the most natural and literal reading of this text only yields an understanding of events that relate to Christ's second coming prior to establishing his millennial kingdom. Any details that would mark this coming of Christ as secret have to be pushed into the text from other places, most notably from Matthew 24:40–41.

Historic Premillennialists emphasize that the context of the apostle Paul's description of the rapture in 1 Thessalonians 4:13–18 seems more in keeping with events related to Christ's final coming rather than to an earlier secret rapture. Consider why Paul wrote these words. After establishing the church in Thessalonica, Paul left the city on a journey to Berea and then Athens and Corinth. During his absence, some of the believers in Thessalonica died, causing great grief and uncertainty in the church. "They evidently did not know what to make of the death of fellow believers before Jesus' return and were distressed about their fate, about which they had not received any teaching. . . . Paul's concern in this passage is to reassure the Christians in Thessalonica that believers who have died will be raised from the dead to join the living believers when Jesus returns."[2]

The apostle seems more concerned with establishing assurance of an eternal reunion with believing loved ones rather than an earthly rescue from the evils of a tribulation that would require another return to earth seven years later. Also, the way Paul ends the text with the phrase "so we will always be with the Lord" (v. 17) seems more about our final destiny than about a temporary or intermediate stage in God's plan.[3]

Finally, Historic Premillennialists object to the claim that this passage supports a secret rapture because the details Paul includes don't seem consistent with the idea of a secret. Verse 16 tells us that the Lord will descend from heaven with a loud command, the voice of an archangel will be heard, and a trumpet will blast. Jesus is coming with a battle cry to defeat the antichrist, Satan, and death. Also, before any living people are caught up in the air to be with Christ, believers who have already died will rise first to meet him, which is bound to draw some attention (vv. 16–17). Finally, when Christ returns to set up his millennial kingdom and rule with his saints over all the earth, the whole world order will change as the antichrist is destroyed, Satan is bound, and evil is restrained across the world.[4] This will be something nobody can or should keep secret.

Of course, traditional Dispensationalists might reasonably ask Historic Premillennialists why any believers are "caught up" in the clouds to meet the Lord if there is no need to remove the church from the earth to advance God's plans for Israel. Why are believers, both dead and alive, "caught up together . . . in the clouds to meet the Lord in the air" if he is on his way down to earth for the final time? Michael Holmes provides this explanation:

> The word for "meeting" . . . was frequently used in secular Greek as a technical term for the formal reception of a visiting dignitary, in which a delegation of citizens or city officials would go out to meet a guest on his way to the city and escort him back into town with appropriate pomp and circumstance. . . . The implication of

Paul's use of this word here is that the resurrected dead and the raptured living together will meet the descending Lord "in the air" and
accompany him in glory and honor the rest of the way to earth.[5]

Thus, the purpose of this rapture scenario isn't to hide a secret
but to honor the Savior.

The upshot of all this back-and-forth discussion about the rapture is that Historic Premillennialists claim that Dispensationalists
presuppose the need for a secret rapture and then find a passage
to support it rather than giving the biblical text its more plain
and natural interpretation. On the other hand, Dispensationalists
reasonably question why there's a need for Christians, alive and
dead, to be raised up into the air if they're coming right back down
to earth. Historic Premillennialists say that a rapture is needed to
usher in the glory of the second coming. Dispensationalists say that
a secret rapture is needed to rescue believers from the tribulation.

The Tribulation and Antichrist

Since Historic Premillennialists don't see the necessity of a secret rapture to rescue Christians from the tribulation, we have
to ask, Do Historic Premillennialists believe in the tribulation?
The answer is yes, but in a different sense than Dispensationalists
anticipate it.[6]

Historic Premillennialists point out that the Greek word *thlipsis*,
meaning "tribulation," occurs forty-five times in the New Testament. In John 16:33 Jesus tells his disciples that they will experience tribulation because they follow him and proclaim the gospel.
In Acts 14:21–22 Paul and Barnabas "returned to Lystra and to
Iconium and to Antioch, strengthening the souls of the disciples,
encouraging them to continue in the faith, and saying that through
many tribulations we must enter the kingdom of God." In other
words, many passages say that those who follow Jesus will regularly experience tribulation.

Faithful Christians should expect to experience tribulation. Christians throughout history suffer, are persecuted, and regularly face the difficulties of a fallen and sinful world. For these reasons, Historic Premillennialists see no reason why believers who have always experienced tribulation should be delivered from a "great tribulation" that precedes the second coming. Both Dispensationalists and Historic Premillennialists agree that the second coming is preceded by a time of some kind of apostasy and suffering (2 Thess. 2:3–4). In this sense, there's clear agreement that believers are rescued from the evil and pain of a period of distress prior to Christ's return (cf. figures 4.1 and 6.1).

However, we must be honest that the Dispensational system is much more dependent upon the events, persons, and length of THE tribulation. For Dispensationalists the pressures of the great tribulation are needed to trigger the conversion of most Jews prior to Christ's second coming. For Historic Premillennialists the prediction of tribulation is needed to prepare the church for the persecutions that inevitably precede Christ's second coming. From this perspective, the great tribulation of Revelation 7:14 need not refer to any period more specific than the collective eras on earth in which Christians have been martyred for their faith.

One of the clear marks of the great tribulation for Dispensationalists is that an antichrist will create great deception and suffering during the time preceding Christ's final return. Many Historic Premillennialists agree that a "man of lawlessness" will dominate a time of persecution and suffering prior to Christ's final return (see 2 Thess. 2:2–12).[7] We are forewarned of this evil for at least three reasons: (1) so we won't expect Christ's second coming prior to this antichrist (vv. 2–3; cf. Matt. 24:23–26); (2) so we won't be surprised or deceived by the antichrist's opposition to the work of the church under a cloak of godliness (vv. 4–7; cf. Matt. 24:15); and (3) so we won't lose hope that Christ will ultimately destroy the antichrist (v. 8; cf. Matt. 24:29–31).[8]

Though many Dispensationalists and Historic Premillennialists agree on the cruelties, deceptions, and ultimate demise of the antichrist, both groups have questions about the nature of the tribulation he causes. For example, they wonder how Jesus can say that the suffering he predicts will accompany the fall of Jerusalem and the destruction of the temple (most likely referencing the events of AD 70) is "never to be equaled again" (Mark 13:19 NIV). Won't suffering during the tribulation that precedes his second coming be even worse?

Craig Blomberg, a professor at Denver Seminary, answers by saying, "For Jesus, then, 'great tribulation' refers neither to the events of the second century BC [when the Greek ruler Antiochus Epiphanes defiled the temple] nor to a period of time only just preceding his return but, at least in part, to the distress at the time of the destruction of Jerusalem, the burning of the city, and the razing of the temple by the Romans in AD 70."[9] In other words, the tribulation Jesus predicts has both a soon (AD 70) and an ultimate (end times) fulfillment. Tribulation is a way of categorizing the distress of believers in times near and far but is not a specific period.

Not all will agree, of course, that Christ's words could have this double meaning—or it's probably fairer to say this immediate and ultimate fulfillment. Still, such interpretation fits with some Historic Premillennial thinking that the Holy Spirit could intend for a prophecy to have a specific and a fuller meaning, especially if tribulation is a general reference to persecution and suffering rather than to a specific period on the prophetic timetable, as when the apostle John indicates we are already in tribulation (Rev. 1:9).[10]

Even if tribulation is usually interpreted as a generic category of suffering, most Historic Premillennialists still believe a more intense period of tribulation will culminate in the return of Jesus and the overthrow of the antichrist.[11] George Eldon Ladd states that in Revelation 19 "[Jesus] comes as 'King of kings and Lord of lords' (Rev. 19:16) to do battle with Antichrist. . . . He will not win his victory by the use of the military weapons of the world but with his bare word. He will speak and the victory will be his."[12]

This glorious picture still leaves us with many questions, but it provides two necessary requirements for biblical faithfulness through the last days: warning and hope.[13] We receive warning to prepare for trial and persecution, and we're given hope to endure with the expectation of Christ's ultimate victory.

The Millennial Kingdom

One key aspect of Christ's victory that brings Dispensationalists and Historic Premillennialists into agreement is the timing of the millennial kingdom. Both think the second coming of Christ will precede a thousand-year reign of God on the earth with his people (cf. figures 4.1 and 6.1). Craig Blomberg asks, "Why am I a premillennialist from a New Testament point of view? Because, no matter how many flashbacks or disruptions of chronological sequence one might want to argue for elsewhere in Revelation, it makes absolutely no sense to put one in between Revelation 19 [describing the victory of Christ's armies over evil] and 20 [describing Christ's thousand-year reign] as both amillennialists and postmillennialists must do."[14]

In other words, the most straightforward reading of Revelation 19 and 20 will show that Christ's victory over evil on this earth comes before the millennium. So, Christ's second coming is premillennial. Historic Premillennialists want to recognize and honor this plain reading of the final chapters in Revelation.[15] However, while such a reading reveals the sequence of events around the millennium, it doesn't tell us much about the nature of this period in which Christ is expected to reign upon the earth.

Some Historic Premillennialists believe the millennium will last a literal thousand years, while others view the thousand years symbolically. New Testament professor Eckhard Schnabel takes the latter view: "Since similar numbers in Jewish texts have a figurative meaning and, more importantly, since many numbers in the book of Revelation are symbolic, it seems probable that the number 'one thousand' is symbolic as well."[16]

What happens during the millennium? Why do we even need it? Why does Jesus need this lengthy time of earthly rule prior to his final judgment of all that is evil? Historic Premillennialists say that during the millennium God will vindicate the rule of Christ. To vindicate means to remove doubt or to prove true. So the millennial rule of Christ first proves true what the prophets of God said. The prophets said that the Messiah would come and establish his kingdom of peace and righteousness (Isa. 11:1–9; Hab. 2:4). Jesus also promised such a kingdom (Matt. 19:28; 24:29–30). So God proves his Word to be true without a doubt by establishing the millennium in which Satan's influences are bound (Rev. 20:1–3) and Christ's rule is complete over all nations and the world's evil (Isa. 2:2–4; 42:1).[17]

Second, God uses the millennium to vindicate believers who have suffered or been martyred for their faith through the ages, including those who have suffered under tribulation prior to Christ's return. All of Christ's followers are proven to be right for their convictions (Rev. 7:13–17). The scales of justice are balanced for the trials and persecutions they have endured as they experience the fullness of Christ's blessings on earth (Rev. 6:10–11; 20:4). In this millennial kingdom, God's people are expected to experience unprecedented happiness, peace, love for one another, and nearness to Christ. In addition, the righteousness of God that has been opposed by the world from its earliest days is shown to be right for his people as they receive the blessings of righteousness that God always promised would be theirs by honoring Christ and his ways.[18]

Believers also rule with Christ during this thousand-year period (Matt. 19:28; Rev. 20:4). The earthly persecutions and suffering they endured from evil powers are shown to be worth it as they dispense a thousand years of Christ's righteousness, peace, and justice. All oppressions and afflictions are counterbalanced by a thousandfold blessing of the believers' millennial reign in Jesus's kingdom (Isa. 65:17–20).

I recently felt the significance of this understanding when a young man poured out his grief at being made a lifelong invalid following a needed brain operation. As a former engineer, he explained his consternation about God's care by drawing a graph of his life on a table napkin. He said, "I understand how the rising blessings you experience after first trusting Jesus can be followed by some troughs of trial and heartache in a fallen world. Yet, if God is really caring for us, then the troughs should be balanced out by later blessings. But when I diagram my life, all I see is a trough that never ends. How can this be true and God be good?"

Perhaps many of you react the way I do when facing hard questions about God's provision in this broken and evil world. I panic inside. I wonder how to answer in a way that will be honest about pain and truthful about God's provision. Yet, in this case I think the Holy Spirit rescued me by helping me respond to the young engineer by saying, "Your timeline is too short. Even if that last trough lasts the rest of your earthly life with no other joys along the way, it will be many times shorter than the blessed existence of the thousandfold blessings that God has in store for you in his kingdom. I don't know why the Lord needs your testimony through suffering today, but I know that this earthly affliction cannot compare to the incomparable and lasting glory of God's kingdom that Jesus has secured for you."

For Historic Premillennialists, such a counterbalance of God's millennial reign isn't simply an abstract concept; it's the sure consolation that believers need to live for Christ through present trials. To be honest, other millennial views that don't include an earthly thousand-year reign of Christ will question why the eternal realities of heaven don't provide the same vindication. But for Dispensationalists and Historic Premillennialists, it's particularly just and fitting that earthly suffering and persecution be righted *on earth* through the rule of Christ and his followers in the millennium.

Historic Premillennialism also teaches that, at the end of the millennium, there's one final trial that believers must face for God to complete his plan for our eternal good. Satan will be released from his bondage so that he can be ultimately and eternally defeated—never more to be feared or to have influence over our world or our hearts. Satan, of course, has no intention of cooperating with this plan. With his release, he will seek to overthrow Christ's kingdom. The battle of Armageddon ensues. Satan loses. Jesus wins. Then the full blessings of eternity are ushered in. These events are largely based on Revelation 20:7–10:

> When the thousand years are ended, Satan will be released from his prison and will come out to deceive the nations that are at the four corners of the earth, Gog and Magog, to gather them for battle; their number is like the sand of the sea. And they marched up over the broad plain of the earth and surrounded the camp of the saints and the beloved city, but fire came down from heaven and consumed them, and the devil who had deceived them was thrown into the lake of fire and sulfur where the beast and the false prophet were, and they will be tormented day and night forever and ever.

After Christ's victory over Satan, the unbelieving dead are resurrected, and there is a final judgment before the great white throne of King Jesus.[19] Satan and those who have served him are cast into an eternal lake of fire along with death and Hades (i.e., the place of the dead, probably meaning the grave). God then provides a new heaven and new earth for the eternal dwelling of those who love him through faith in Jesus Christ.

The New Heaven and Earth

Although many Christians think that we'll spend eternity as disembodied souls in an ethereal heaven, Historic Premillennialists (and most other views represented in this book) believe that God will establish a new heaven and earth for the eternal blessing of his people (Rev. 21:1). Believers will experience eternity on an earth made perfect. The world that was marked by corruption, war, disease, trials, and pain will pass away. We will be granted eternal souls and perfected bodies to experience the fullness of God's blessings physically and spiritually on earth. In Revelation 21:3–4 John describes what life in this restored creation will be like:

> Behold, the dwelling place of God is with man. He will dwell with them, and they will be his people, and God himself will be with them as their God. He will wipe away every tear from their eyes, and death shall be no more, neither shall there be mourning, nor crying, nor pain anymore, for the former things have passed away.

Revelation 22:1–5 provides even greater detail of this eternal home:

> Then the angel showed me the river of the water of life, bright as crystal, flowing from the throne of God and of the Lamb through the middle of the street of the city; also, on either side of the river, the tree of life with its twelve kinds of fruit, yielding its fruit each month. The leaves of the tree were for the healing of the nations. No longer will there be anything accursed, but the throne of God and of the Lamb will be in it, and his servants will worship him. They will see his face, and his name will be on their foreheads. And night will be no more. They will need no light of lamp or

sun, for the Lord God will be their light, and they will reign forever and ever.

The end times will be followed by eternity. There our bodies and souls will experience the absence of sin's effects on our existence as well as the intimate and unobstructed presence of Christ's blessings, power, and love forever. On these matters we agree and rejoice.

Amillennial View

Amillennialists believe the *spiritual* realities of the millennium kingdom are already present (see description in chap. 3). Although the prefix *a-* (meaning "no" or "without") might be thought to indicate that there's no millennium in this interpretation of Scripture, that isn't the case. Amillennialists believe Christ's millennial reign has already begun and will continue through the time of his second coming. Amillennialists believe in a *now* millennium. For them, Christ's kingdom was inaugurated with the events of his cross and resurrection that provide for the defeat of Satan in our hearts immediately and in our world eventually. The events of history are unfolding like a cornucopia of grace, with the spiritual realities of Christ's kingdom progressing and expanding according to God's mission for gathering and blessing his people (see the spiral representing the grace of God in figure 8.1).

A Cornucopia of Grace Perspective

Amillennialists don't ignore Scripture to take this spiritual viewpoint but rather point to statements by Jesus, such as "The kingdom of God is not coming in ways that can be observed, nor will

Figure 8.1
Amillennial View of the End Times

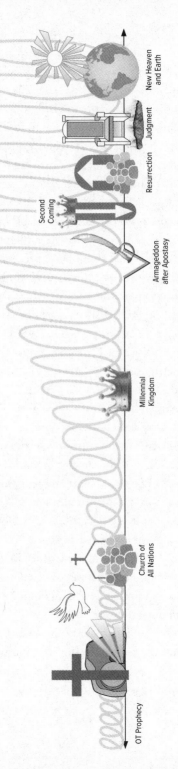

Increasing fulfillment of prophetic prediction and Christ's kingdom purposes.

they say, 'Look, here it is!' or 'There!' for behold, the kingdom of God is in the midst of you" (Luke 17:20–22).

The idea that the kingdom of God isn't so much about physical land, armies, temples, and beasts but about Christ's rule in our hearts can gain further support from the apostle Paul's words: "For the kingdom of God is not a matter of eating and drinking but of righteousness and peace and joy in the Holy Spirit" (Rom. 14:17). Paul also says that God "has delivered us from the domain of darkness and transferred us to the kingdom of his beloved Son" (Col. 1:13). Such statements suggest that the millennial kingdom isn't primarily a future, physical realm but a present, spiritual reality.

To appreciate how different this view is from the Premillennial views, we might compare our present world to a description of the millennium by popular Dispensationalist author and preacher Dr. David Jeremiah: "Can you imagine a world with no fear? No disease? No pain? No worry. That's what the Millennial Kingdom will be like. For a thousand years, there will be peace—we will live in a perfect world with Christ as our ruler. . . . All the hostilities that have been part of our world will be gone."[1] Sounds wonderful, doesn't it? It provides a hopeful contrast to our current sinful world that's full of heartache, disappointment, and tragedy. It certainly doesn't sound like our present world.

That's why it can be so shocking to hear that Amillennialists believe we're living in the millennium now. Are they delusional? Don't they watch the daily news? Let me quickly respond with an emphatic "no"—they aren't delusional. And yes, they're fully aware of the world we live in. As we will see in this chapter, Amillennialists believe that Premillennialists have seriously misunderstood the nature and timing of the millennium. How did we get so far apart in understanding?

Although Premillennialism was the primary view of the early church, that changed dramatically due to Saint Augustine of Hippo (AD 354–430). In his book *City of God*, Augustine taught that the binding of Satan began with the first coming of Christ. Christ's resurrection and ascension marked the victory over sin and Satan that would provide the most important blessings of the kingdom and culminate in Jesus's second coming. Augustine's view eventually won the day, and it became the dominant view among Christians from that time to the present. Even John Walvoord, former president of the Dispensational Dallas Theological Seminary, admits the following:

> Because amillennialism was adopted by the Reformers, it achieved a quality of orthodoxy to which its modern adherents can point with pride. They can rightly claim many worthy scholars in the succession from the Reformation to modern times such as Calvin, Luther, Melanchthon, and in modern times, Warfield, Vos, Kuyper, Machen, and Berkhof. If one follows traditional Reformed theology in many other aspects, it is natural to accept its amillennialism. The weight of organized Christianity has largely been on the side of amillennialism.[2]

Old Testament Prophecy

As we saw in chapter 4, traditional Dispensationalists believe that all other views spiritualize Old Testament prophecies rather than interpreting them literally. Amillennialists disagree with this characterization that suggests they arbitrarily shift meaning from specific to symbolic interpretations. Instead, Amillennialists claim that we should view Old Testament prophecies as the Holy Spirit has directed through the lens of the New Testament. Amillennialists say that rather than being arbitrary, this approach binds us to Scripture's intent.

Robert Strimple, professor emeritus of systematic theology at Westminster Seminary California, writes,

> All evangelical Christians are accustomed to viewing the Old Testament sacrifices and feasts and ceremonies as being types, that is, teaching tools pointing forward to the work of Christ.

Why then should the elements that we will consider now—the land of Canaan, the city of Jerusalem, the temple, the throne of David, the nation of Israel itself—not be understood using the same interpretive insight that we use in interpreting the sacrifices and ceremonies?[3]

In other words, Amillennialists believe the proper contrast isn't between literal and spiritual interpretation. Instead, the contrast is between shadow and reality, promise and fulfillment. This perspective understands the New Testament to be teaching us how we should interpret the Old Testament prophecies in the way that it shows us how Christ fulfilled the symbols and types that prefigured him. The Old Testament types, such as the sacrifices, feasts, temple, and land, are shadows of the reality that will be fulfilled in Christ. So when the reality comes, the shadows pass away. Such shadows are not to be restored in the future because they have been entirely fulfilled in Christ.[4]

To be more specific, from the perspective of Amillennialists the Old Testament sacrifices were a shadow, and Christ's death on the cross is the reality. The Old Testament temple was the shadow of the true temple, which is Jesus and those who belong to him (John 2:19–22; 1 Cor. 3:16–17; Eph. 2:19–22). Likewise, the land of Canaan was merely a shadow of the much fuller reality of the new heaven and earth promised to Abraham's true "seed"—Jesus Christ and those united to him (Gal. 3:16). Amillennialists say that if we insist on viewing all the Old Testament prophecies and promises *literally* (as Dispensationalists define that term), then we'll miss the *literary* directions the Holy Spirit provided in the New Testament to reveal their fulfillment in Christ.

The Church Age

Since Amillennialists see the New Testament as fulfilling the intentions of God that were set in motion in the Old Testament, the division of God's purposes and people as taught in the Dispensational view are unnecessary. They believe the concept of a church age, in which God's dealings with Israel pause while he implements a different plan to save a new group known as the church, is foreign to Scripture and to the nature of God's redemptive plan for all people.

Amillennialists embrace a Covenantal view of the Bible that understands God to reveal his salvation plan through successive covenants that progressively display the nature and extent of his grace (see the following sidebar). All of history and humanity are addressed by this unified plan. From the dawn of humanity God's intention was to provide a Redeemer so that all nations would be saved by faith in his grace to fulfill the unfolding promises made to Adam, Noah, Abraham, Moses, and David (e.g., Gen. 3:15; 9:15–17; 15:6; 17:5). Amillennialists do not share the view that Israel and the church must be kept separate in God's plan, nor do any other of the most historic Christian views of the end times.

A Covenantal View of the Bible

God reveals his salvation plan through unfolding covenants of grace that culminate in the ministry of Jesus Christ for climactic completion in the eternal kingdom.

⟶ **GRACE from eternity past**
revealed through the covenants with
Adam → Noah → Abraham → Moses → David → Christ
providing eternal blessings of
GRACE into eternity future ⟶

How, then, do Amillennialists view the relationship between Israel and the church? Robert Strimple explains:

> We say: "Yes, the nation of Israel was the people of God in the
> old covenant. Now in the new covenant the believing church is the
> people of God." . . . Christians are the Israel of God, Abraham's
> seed, and the heirs of the promises, only because by faith we are
> united to him who is alone the true Israel, Abraham's one seed
> (note Paul's emphasis on the singular in Gal. 3:16).[5]

Some critics have viewed this position as *replacement theology*,
which is the view that the Old Testament entity known as Israel
has now been replaced by the church. "This suggests that wherever
the word 'Israel' is used in the Bible it now refers to the Church,
for the Church is the inheritor of all the blessings and promises
given to the Jewish people."[6] But Amillennialists would claim that
this doesn't truly represent their view. (See a similar rejection of
this terminology by Historic Premillennialists in the discussion of
adoption and engrafting in chap. 6).

As stated above, Amillennialists believe the New Testament
teaches that all the promises God made to Israel are now fulfilled
in their Messiah, Jesus Christ. In the Old Testament, the Lord
refers to Israel as a "vine" (Ps. 80:8–15; Isa. 5:1–7; Jer. 2:21). But
in the New Testament, Jesus declares, "I am the true vine" (John
15:1). In other words, Jesus claims that he is the true Israel. So all
who are united to him by faith, whether Jew or gentile, become
Abraham's children and heirs of God's promises (Gal. 3:15–29).

The promises made to Israel haven't been annulled or replaced
but expanded to include not only believing Israel but also believing
gentiles. Strimple writes that Premillennialists have often asked,
"But what about 'the hope of Israel'? Does not the amillennialist
understanding of biblical revelation rob Israel of her hope?"[7] His
answer is no, the hope of Israel is the spiritual status that all of
God's elect share by faith in Christ—the elect of Israel as well as the
elect of the gentiles. Thus, figure 8.1 shows the spiral representing
the grace of God progressing throughout the Old Testament and
expanding into New Testament promises and eternal provision.

The Rapture

Amillennialists don't believe in a secret rapture of the church prior to the second coming of Christ. Instead, along with all millennial views except Dispensational Premillennialism, Amillennialists believe the rapture will occur at the same time as Christ's second coming. At that time all who are part of the church—both living and dead, Jew and gentile—will meet him in the air. Dr. Sam Storms, a highly respected pastor who graduated from Dallas Theological Seminary in 1977, explains how books by Historic Premillennialist George Ladd and Amillennialists Anthony Hoekema and Robert Gundry changed his perspective about the rapture:

> It wasn't long before Ladd, Hoekema, and Gundry, together with a few others, had persuaded me that there is no basis in Scripture for a pre-tribulational rapture of the church. That was, in the eyes of many, bad enough. Indeed, I distinctly recall the horror (trust me, "horror" is by no means an exaggerated term to describe the reaction I received) in my church when I made it known that I could no longer embrace a pre-tribulation rapture. More than a few were convinced that I was well on my way into theological liberalism![8]

What, specifically, in these books and in the New Testament convinced Storms that his former views were wrong? Among other things, he came to believe that the rapture and the second coming of Christ will occur at the same time, not seven years apart. He writes:

> The return of Christ at the close of history is a singular, unitary event. There is no such thing as a rapture or translation or catching up into heaven of the Church before the time known as the great tribulation, to be followed, at the tribulation's close, by yet another "return" of Christ to judge and destroy his enemies. Jesus will descend from heaven but once, at which time he will rapture and resurrect his Church to be with him forever. But he will not then

return into the clouds of heaven but will continue his descent and destroy his enemies, thereby bringing human history to its close, after which is the creation of the new heavens and new earth (what we typically refer to as the eternal state).[9]

Storms clearly states that, like the other views presented in this book, Amillennialism teaches that a rapture will take place. But unlike Dispensationalists, whose views dominate popular books and movies, Amillennialists believe the rapture will occur at the time of Christ's second coming, not prior to the tribulation. As indicated earlier, all four views include a time of intensified persecution and pain prior to Christ's return, but only the Dispensational view specifies a seven-year period of tribulation following a secret rapture and preceding the millennial kingdom.

The Tribulation and Second Coming

Amillennialists agree with Historic Premillennialists about the nature and duration of tribulation experiences. Both believe that the church will endure tribulation and suffering during the period between Christ's first and second comings. According to Amillennialists, however, these aren't the events of a specific seven-year period dominated by the antichrist and concluded by Armageddon. Rather, the tribulation of this present millennium includes the afflictions and persecutions that Christians around the world regularly experience.

Amillennialists support this perspective by pointing to New Testament passages such as 2 Timothy 3:12–13, where Paul writes, "Indeed, all who desire to live a godly life in Christ Jesus will be persecuted, while evil people and impostors will go from bad to worse, deceiving and being deceived" (see also John 15:19–20; 1 Pet. 4:12–14; Rev. 1:9). Richard Gaffin, who was a professor at Westminster Theological Seminary from 1999 to 2008, writes, "Over the interadventual period [that is, the time between Christ's birth and second coming] in its entirety, from beginning to end, a fundamental aspect of the church's existence is (to be) 'suffering with Christ'; nothing, the New Testament teaches, is more basic to its identity than that."[10]

Amillennialists also link much of the church's suffering throughout history to antichrists that are not the spectacular monsters of the movies, the national opponents of our politics, or the religious antagonists to our faith. They may, in fact, be all of these—and more. After all, the apostle John taught us, "Every spirit that does not confess Jesus is not from God. This is the spirit of the antichrist, which you heard was coming and now is in the world already" (1 John 4:3). Earlier in his letter John adds, "Children, it is the last hour, and as you have heard that antichrist is coming, so now many antichrists have come. Therefore we know that it is the last hour" (2:18). Since we know that we're already in the end times (on "the last hour," see chap. 1), John's words lead Amillennialists to believe that ever since Jesus ascended there have been antichrists in every generation in the form of the prevailing evil of our age (2 John 1:7).

Still, it's important not to make generic evil the only way we identify the antichrist. Important voices among Amillennialists join with the most credible proponents of other views to warn of an ultimate and specific expression of the antichrist prior to the Lord's return. The apostle Paul gives good reason for this:

> The lawless one will be revealed, whom the Lord Jesus will kill with the breath of his mouth and bring to nothing by the appearance of his coming. The coming of the lawless one is by the activity of Satan with all power and false signs and wonders, and with all wicked deception for those who are perishing, because they refused to love the truth and so be saved. (2 Thess. 2:8–10)

Of course, any person, institution, or idea that opposes Jesus Christ possesses what John calls "the spirit of the antichrist."

But Amillennialists also recognize that there's an intensifying of the personification of evil in biblical passages that describe the lead-up to Christ's return (Matt. 24:24–28; 2 Thess. 2:1–3; Rev. 19:19–20).

We do not know the precise nature and name of the antichrist. But the patterns of his activity and evil are signaled throughout Scripture so that God's people are appropriately warned in every age to prepare for his deceits and Christ's return (Dan. 7:8, 19–25; 9:26–27; Matt. 24:24; Mark 13:6, 22; Rev. 13:1). In his book *A Case for Amillennialism*, Kim Riddlebarger writes,

> It is my contention that Christ's church will face two significant threats associated with the Antichrist. The first of these threats is internal—a series of antichrists who arise within the church and are tied to a particular heresy, the denial that Jesus Christ is God in human flesh. This internal threat has been present since the days of the apostles in the form of various heresies and will be present until the time of the end when Jesus Christ returns. The second threat is external—the repeated manifestation of the mysterious beast throughout the course of history (as depicted in the book of Revelation), taking the form of state-sponsored heresy and the persecution of Christ's church and the people of God.[11]

Many Amillennialists believe that John's description of the two beasts in Revelation 13—the beast from the sea and the beast from the earth—refers to the Roman Empire and its imperial cult that deified and worshiped the emperor Nero. He persecuted Christians, executed Peter and Paul, and blamed Christians for the fire that nearly destroyed Rome.[12] But that doesn't mean that Nero was the ultimate antichrist. Riddlebarger explains that "various beasts (governments) and their leaders and henchmen will come and go until one final manifestation of satanic rage and deception breaks out, immediately before the Lord returns."[13]

The Millennial Kingdom

As I mentioned at the beginning of this chapter, Amillennialists believe we're in the millennium now. How do they arrive at this conclusion? The answer, in part, is found in the way they interpret the book of Revelation. Anthony Hoekema (1913–1988), who was professor of systematic theology at Calvin Theological Seminary and an Amillennialist, admits that if the millennium events described in Revelation 20 "must necessarily follow, in chronological order" the events of Christ's second coming described in chapter 19, then we are "virtually compelled to believe that the thousand-year reign depicted in 20:4 must come after the return of Christ described in 19:11."[14] In other words, Hoekema acknowledges that simply taking these chapters in the sequence they appear in Scripture would produce a Premillennial perspective rather than an Amillennial one.

But, in fact, Hoekema and other Amillennialists don't believe that what John describes in Revelation 20:1–4 was intended to follow chronologically after the events of Revelation 19. Instead, they think the binding of Satan described in those verses occurred during Jesus's earthly ministry and crucifixion. And the thousand-year reign of Christ mentioned in Revelation 20 refers to the entire period between his first and second comings. How can this chronology be justified if it isn't the sequence of the Revelation chapters?

Amillennialists base their conclusions on a view of Revelation known as *progressive parallelism*. Hoekema explains that this view sees the book of Revelation as consisting of seven sections that are parallel to each other. Each section reprises the interactions of the church and the world from the time of Christ's first coming until the time of his second coming.[15] If this is correct, the book of Revelation doesn't depict events in a strict sequence from first to last but rather gives us different perspectives on the same events as they are cycled before us in the seven sections. Each perspective serves different purposes and adds fuller understanding for worshiping God's glory, preparing God's people, encouraging Christ's church, and warning Christ's enemies. In essence, Amillennialists claim Revelation repeats seven versions of the same movie that often cover the same time period but are filmed from different angles.

The seven sections that Amillennialists see for the cycles of Revelation are as follows:

1. The letter to the seven churches (Rev. 1–3)
2. The vision of the seven seals (Rev. 4–7)
3. The seven trumpets of judgment (Rev. 8–11)
4. The woman and the dragon (Rev. 12–14)
5. The seven bowls of wrath (Rev. 15–16)
6. The fall of Babylon and of the beasts (Rev. 17–19)
7. The doom of the dragon, the final judgment, the triumph of Christ and his church, and the new heaven and earth (Rev. 20–22)

Is there any basis for concluding that these sections may be cyclical rather than sequential? Amillennialists will point out that Revelation 11 concludes with the second coming of Christ, but Revelation 12 starts over with the birth of Christ. Those two chapters are obviously not chronological or sequential. Rather, they seem to be reprising aspects of God's glory so that those facing future persecutions are aided by a reminder of God's past providences. John takes his readers to the climax of Christ's return, then backs up to remind them that, since God has been victorious over evil before, there's no reason to doubt him now. Similar reasoning could explain why Christ's return is described so vividly in Revelation 1 before we read of the frailties and faults of the churches in Revelation 2–3.

Amillennialists see these separate sections variously cycling through history and prophecy, wisdom and warning, cautions to heed and hope to note. Therefore, Amillennialists don't see that Revelation 19 and 20 must be considered in a sequential order if they're parts of separate sections—chapter 19 ending one cycle and chapter 20 beginning another cycle. Such a view of Revelation 19 and 20 allows interpreters to conclude that the millennium doesn't come after the second coming, even if that's the order of the material in the chapters.

Even if this progressive parallelism is a valid way of looking at Revelation, how can Amillennialists claim that the binding of Satan and the millennium began at Christ's first coming? Strimple explains that the first coming of Christ was an "anticipatory consummation."[16] By his death and resurrection, Jesus won the decisive battle over Satan. The final results of that battle are yet to come when Christ returns to establish the glory of his eternal kingdom. Still, because Christ has already fought with Satan and won, there is a real sense in which the kingdom of God has already come.

Amillennialists point to a number of New Testament passages that claim Satan was "bound," "cast out," and "disarmed" during the earthly ministry of Jesus:

> If it is by the Spirit of God that I [Jesus] cast out demons, then the kingdom of God has come upon you. Or how can someone enter a strong man's house and plunder his goods, unless he first binds the strong man? (Matt. 12:28–29)

> Now is the judgment of this world; now will the ruler of this world be cast out. (John 12:31)

> He [Jesus] disarmed the rulers and authorities and put them to open shame, by triumphing over them in him. (Col. 2:15)

Strimple clarifies what it means for Satan to be bound during the time between Christ's first and second coming: "At the cross Satan is bound—but not absolutely. Revelation 20:2–3 does not say that Satan is bound, period. He is bound in one respect only, namely, 'to keep him from deceiving the nations [the Gentiles] anymore.'"[17] As a consequence, the cross commences the age of world missions, the gospel spreads across the earth, and the absolute sway that Satan had over all nations but Israel came to an end with Christ's resurrection and ascension.

Of course, the fact that Jesus bound, cast out, and disarmed Satan doesn't mean the evil one is no longer active in this present world. Obviously he is, as the rest of the New Testament makes clear. Instead, Jesus's triumph over Satan and his forces was like the D-day invasion, which was a decisive victory that was the beginning of the end of World War II. In one sense the war was already won by the events of D-day; in another sense the fighting was yet to be concluded. The victory was *already* won, but the full reality was *not yet*. So also are the realities of the millennial kingdom for Amillennialists. They say that we're already in the millennium until the total victory and celebration of Christ's second coming, which has yet to happen.

Theologian Douglas Kelly offers these important insights supporting an Amillennial perspective and offering an explanation for the time frame of a spiritual millennium that other perspectives expect to last a literal thousand years:

> How long does the millennium last? There can be no doubt that it began with the completed work of Christ on earth. Revelation 20 [describing the Millennium] follows immediately upon Revelation 19, which celebrates the triumph of the One who is "King of kings and Lord of lords" (v. 16). . . . But when does it end? Revelation 20 presents it as continuing until the end of the age, when after a brief uprising by Satan, the final judgment takes place (20:7–11). That means that the evil one is bound from deceiving the nations until just before the conclusion of salvation history.[18]

Amillennialists point to other New Testament passages to show that the kingdom of God has already been put in effect by the earthly ministry of Jesus:

136

The time is fulfilled, and the kingdom of God is at hand; repent and believe in the gospel. (Mark 1:15)

He said to them, "Truly, I say to you, there are some standing here who will not taste death until they see the kingdom of God after it has come with power." (Mark 9:1)

Heal the sick in it and say to them, "The kingdom of God has come near to you." (Luke 10:9)

Giving thanks to the Father, who has qualified you to share in the inheritance of the saints in light. He has delivered us from the domain of darkness and transferred us to the kingdom of his beloved Son, in whom we have redemption, the forgiveness of sins. (Col. 1:12–14)

Is the kingdom of God in these passages the same as THE millennial kingdom? Amillennialists would say yes. They see the book of Revelation as full of symbolic language and images, so the thousand years referred to in Revelation 20 doesn't need to be interpreted as an exact thousand years. Instead, as mentioned previously, it describes the period between the first and second comings of Christ when the influence of Satan is so limited that the gospel can progress in our hearts (Rom. 6:6, 14; 1 John 4:4) and among the nations (Matt. 24:14). But if it's an inexact period, why does the Bible talk about a thousand years? Again, Douglas Kelly is helpful:

Why, then, does Revelation use the expression *a thousand years*? In terms of biblical numbers, ten represents fullness, and a thousand is ten times ten times ten, hence fullness times fullness times fullness. It seems to equal a vast number of years without being a precise chronology of human history. Nowhere else does Scripture limit the binding of Satan and the success of the church's mission to a specific period of time before the end of the age. . . . It is not a matter of literally one thousand years, but of God's secret timing as to the gathering of His people into union with Christ, however long that may take from our human perspective.[19]

There's one more important point to mention that convinces Amillennialists that Christ won't have a literal, physical thousand-year reign on earth *after* he returns. They believe the preponderance of evidence in the New Testament doesn't support such a view. They see the New Testament ruling out the notion of an earthly millennial kingdom after Christ's return because it lumps together the second coming of Christ, the resurrection of believers and unbelievers (with judgment for all—believers to eternal life and unbelievers to eternal punishment), the end of our current reality, and the establishment of the eternal realities of the new heaven and earth.[20]

In other words, Amillennialists understand that the entire New Testament—except for ten verses in Revelation 20—says nothing about Christ reigning on an unrenewed earth for a thousand years after he returns. But what about those ten verses in Revelation? Strimple answers with the standard rule of Bible interpretation, saying that clearer Bible passages should determine the meaning of those less clear—and not vice versa. He concludes by questioning whether we should use a single, brief passage that is full of symbols and figurative language to reinterpret the end-times teaching of the rest of the New Testament.[21]

Amillennialists would answer with a firm no.

The New Heaven and Earth

Since Amillennialists don't believe there will be a millennial kingdom immediately following Christ's return, what do they think will happen? As previously said, the just and the unjust will be resurrected and judged. Then the Lord will create a new heaven and earth where he will dwell with his people forever. This means that the events of the last days that climax prior to the second coming of Jesus immediately precede Christ's establishment of the blessings of our eternal home.

After Jesus returns, nothing intervenes before our Lord rescues all believers from the evil of this world. They're immediately taken to be with their Savior for the eternal blessings of the new heaven and new earth. All evil is judged. All those justified by faith in the blood of the Lamb live eternally with restored bodies and purified souls in perfect love, unity, and peace in that place where there's no more darkness, pain, or tears. There we will live forever in the light and love of Jesus.

9

Postmillennial View

The 1900 world's fair held in Paris, France, was known as the Universal Exposition. The fair ran from April to November and was designed to celebrate the achievements of the previous century and to encourage further progress in the twentieth century. More than fifty million people from around the world attended to see such marvels as a moving sidewalk, electric cars, diesel engines, and talking films. These advances in science and culture both reflected and fueled a pervasive optimism people felt about the future of their world.

That optimism colored much Christian thinking as well. In the United States, the Civil War was past. Families and regions were reunited. Wars were distant. Major revivals of faith had brightened the outlook and increased the membership of many churches. Industrial and scientific advances had improved the lives of many (though not all) so that religion became less about relief from desperation and more about investment in and enjoyment of life's opportunities.

A sign of the optimistic attitude of this age came in 1900 when a significant church magazine, *The Christian Oracle*, was renamed

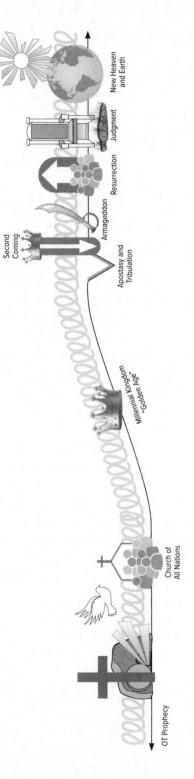

Figure 9.1

Postmillennial View of the End Times

OT Prophecy

Church of All Nations

Millennial Kingdom "Golden Age"

Second Coming

Apostasy and Tribulation

Armageddon

Resurrection

Judgment

New Heaven and Earth

Increasing influence of Christ's kingdom to fulfill prophetic prediction and God's purposes.

The Christian Century. The title identified religious leaders' expectations that they would soon be chronicling a revolutionary harmony of faith and technology that would usher in a new era of unprecedented understanding, prosperity, and peace. This anticipated "Christian" century had all the marks of the long-promised kingdom of God, and churches throughout our nation and world were filled with optimism for the future.

Then the unthinkable happened. The First World War broke out in 1914, and over nine million people died in combat with another five million civilian casualties. Then the Spanish flu epidemic spread in four waves between 1918 and 1920, and an estimated fifty million people died as a result. Although World War I was thought to be "the war to end all wars," that optimistic assessment was subsequently dashed by the Nazi war machine. World War II, the genocide of the Jewish people, the rise of the Soviet Union, the threats of Communist China, and the ensuing Cold War that put the entire world under the threat of a nuclear holocaust—all combined to make optimism about the world's future a quaint memory of past naïveté.

Major conflicts and crises of the twentieth century then carried into the twenty-first with wars in the Middle East, new Russian and Chinese aggressions, African famines, worldwide pandemics, energy crises, economic woes, natural disasters, and mass migrations of refugees. All have served to further extinguish the religious optimism that most churches embraced at the beginning of the twentieth century. We struggle to remember that the predominant perspective of Bible-believing churches through most of America's history was that the world would get better and better under the influence of Christ. How did such a perspective gain a foothold, and what is its status now?

Before and after the Universal Exposition in Paris, there was a common understanding of how the end times would unfold known as Postmillennialism. Proponents of this view believe that Christ will return after the influence of his church has spread across the world, improving the human condition both spiritually and materially. As Christianity progresses, Postmillennialists expect there will also be inevitable and accompanying forces of righteousness, wisdom, and love that will culminate in a so-called golden age of peace and prosperity for a thousand years. Most believe that time frame is a figurative expression for Christ's millennial kingdom. Still, the idyllic features of this millennium that God promised in the Old and New Testaments are expected to dominate this golden age.

After this millennium, Jesus Christ is expected to return to an earth populated mostly by Christians, who through their faith and obedience have prepared for him (ushered him in) by removing most of the world's evils. That's why Postmillennialists expect the world to get better and better and why advances in culture, economics, and technology (especially in Western societies) seemed to confirm these church leaders' anticipation of a better tomorrow.

Through most of its early years, our nation and its churches perceived history to be on an upward trajectory toward the fulfillment of heavenly prophecies. Because of the carnage and crises of the twentieth and twenty-first centuries, much of this optimism has been dashed. Most people have abandoned or forgotten about Postmillennialism—but not all! It has been sustained by those who tell us not to look for the golden age on a near horizon. Instead, they expect the millennial kingdom of biblical prophecy to be a distant future consequence of the gradual but persistent progress of the church as it motors on an uphill climb through a fallen world. Optimism remains but with a long view of the church's future triumph gained over time and on a hill far away.

American theologian and author Loraine Boettner (1901–1990) gave the following summary of Postmillennialism:

A Hill Climb
Perspective

143

Postmillennialism is the view of the last things which holds that the kingdom of God is now being extended in the world through the preaching of the gospel and the saving work of the Holy Spirit in the hearts of individuals, that the world eventually is to be Christianized and that the return of Christ is to occur at the close of a long period of righteousness and peace commonly called the millennium.[1]

Because Postmillennialism has some different features from the other views presented in this book, I'll use some different categories to explain more of its distinctives.

Key Aspects and Figures of Postmillennialism

Key aspects of Postmillennialism first appeared during the Protestant Reformation. Significant passages in Romans 11 (such as verses 23–24 and 28–32) convinced many Reformers that there would eventually be a revival of the Jewish people that followed the great extension of God's grace to gentiles. In their opinion, this revival would usher in a great triumph—a golden age—of Christianity.[2] This expectation created important foundations for the Postmillennial convictions of American advocates whose faith had roots in the Reformation.

An important defense and description of Postmillennialism came from Jonathan Edwards (1703–1758), whom many consider to be America's greatest theologian. As Steven R. Pointer explains,

> Edwards envisioned the Millennium as the church's "triumphant state," a time of Sabbath rest and peace. He expected it to be a time of great advance in knowledge "when neither divine nor human learning shall be confined and imprisoned within only two or three nations of Europe, but shall be diffused all over the world." He looked forward to a time of great holiness when "visible wickedness shall be suppressed everywhere, and true holiness shall become general, though not universal," and a time of great prosperity. He

regarded Constantine's era a type of the greater reality to come, so he also expected the Millennium to be a time when true religion would be held in great esteem and saints would rule on all fronts.[3]

Just as Cold War events would later seem to confirm Dispensational views of the end times, the growth and prosperity of the American colonies combined with the massive spiritual revivals that surrounded the Great Awakening signaled for Edwards and others the optimistic culmination of a Postmillennial worldview. The "usual" absence of war in the Americas, the rise of democracies in Europe, improved lifestyles aided by scientific age precursors, and above all the liveliness and consensus of the Christian faith in the United States and England led most Bible-believing churches in the late eighteenth century and nineteenth century to embrace Postmillennialism.

Even until the late 1920s, the top theologians at Princeton advocated for Postmillennialism. These included Archibald Alexander (1772–1851), who founded Princeton Theological Seminary in 1812; his son Joseph Addison Alexander (1809–1861); Charles Hodge (1797–1878), who was one of the most influential theologians of the nineteenth century in America; his son Archibald Alexander Hodge (1823–1886); and Benjamin Breckinridge Warfield (1851–1921), who was perhaps the greatest of the Princetonians.

A. A. Hodge's response to the question "What is the Scriptural doctrine concerning the millennium?" provides one of the most articulate and specific definitions of Postmillennialism:

1. "The Scriptures . . . clearly reveal that the gospel is to exercise an influence over all branches of the human family, immeasurably more extensive and more thoroughly transforming than any it has ever realized in time past."

2. "The period of this general prevalency of the gospel will continue a thousand years, and is hence designated the millennium (Rev. 20:2–7)."

3. "The Jews are to be converted to Christianity either at
   the commencement or during the continuance of this
   period."
4. "At the end of these thousand years, and before the coming of Christ, there will be a comparatively short season
   of apostasy and violent conflict between the kingdoms of
   light and darkness."
5. "Christ's advent, the general resurrection and judgment,
   will be simultaneous, and immediately succeeded by the
   burning of the old, and the revelation of the new earth
   and heavens."[4]

Following the Fundamentalist-Modernist controversy of the
1920s, Princeton Seminary shifted to a more liberal view of the
Bible that was less concerned about millennial doctrines relating
to Christ's physical return. But prior to that time, this bastion of
biblical orthodoxy and Reformed theology was also a lighthouse
of Postmillennial hopefulness.

In more recent times, some of the best-known supporters of
Postmillennialism include those who root their theology in Refor-
mation distinctions similar to Edwards and the early Princetonians.
These include Loraine Boettner, Kenneth L. Gentry, and D. James
Kennedy, who served for forty-seven years as senior minister of
Coral Ridge Presbyterian Church in Fort Lauderdale, Florida.
Each of these names also signals ways in which Postmillennialism
provided a basis for worldviews whose optimism had significantly
different flavors.

Loraine Boettner, as indicated previously, understood Postmillennialism much as Edwards did—that is, as a *spiritual* movement
whereby the world is gradually Christianized by the preaching
of the Word and the suppression of evil through the work of the
Holy Spirit in the hearts of his people. Ken Gentry, Greg Bahnsen,
Rousas John Rushdoony, Gary North, and others associated with

movements variously identified as Theonomy, Federal Vision, and Christian Reconstructionism, believed that the spiritual changes should be accompanied by *societal* changes such as those that were spelled out in the Old Testament laws for the establishment of a theocratic state. The golden age in this version of Postmillennialism would involve Scripture influencing civil society in ways that make it much like ancient Israel.

D. James Kennedy was also concerned for civil society but focused more on correcting the moral decline of America by having *political* powers acting and ruling according to Christian principles. Kennedy's concern for the exercise of righteous political power put him in league with those of very different theological traditions who had similar political interests. During the Moral Majority movements of the 1970s and 1980s, Pentecostal and Charismatic leaders such as Pat Robertson, who wanted to rescue America from secularizing influences, adopted Postmillennial perspectives that sought to have a Christian society dominated and corrected by the power of the Holy Spirit. For these leaders, the golden age would be when "God's house and God's people are given their rightful place of leadership at the top of the world."[5]

As Postmillennialism morphed into these civil and political expressions in the late twentieth century, it began to influence the wider church with echoes of its past prominence. Nineteenth-century advocates had preached that advances toward the golden age required serious dedication of the church to reforms and revivals in the present age. Revivalist Charles Finney asserted, "If the church will do her duty, the Millennium may come in this country in three years."[6] Such views not only created mission zeal and optimism that the vast majority of the world would be saved prior to Christ's return but also stimulated social reforms against slavery and child labor as well as movements for women's suffrage, universal education, and temperance.

The clear message was that the church needed to get busy to usher in Christ's kingdom. Any millennial view that suggested we can passively wait for the Savior's return to rescue us from the world's problems would lead to the church's abdication of its responsibility. Famous preachers of the nineteenth century, such as Lyman Beecher and Joseph Berg, saw America's reforms as the firstfruits of Christ's kingdom. Their views are echoed in statements of present Christian nationalists who oppose Dispensational and Historic Premillennialists whose end-times emphasis on Christ's rescue from this present evil age are presumed to lead to "an eschatology of defeat."[7] Some of these newer Postmillennialists argue that the pervasiveness of Dispensational views about "the late great planet earth" and "leaving the world behind" have led many in the church to become resigned to our culture's ills and are, at least in part, responsible for its moral decline.

Present Postmillennialists frequently embrace the hopefulness of a Christianized world with the expectation that "we are in the last of the last days."[8] This may sound like what a lot of Dispensationalists say. However, this Postmillennial expectation assumes that the hill climb toward Christ's kingdom began long ago, when Satan took control of the world at the fall of humanity, and that all subsequent moral, cultural, and spiritual progress has occurred only when God's servants have been zealously committed to his Word and will. So if we're in the last of the last days, and if Christ's return must be preceded by a period of apostasy,[9] then the church must be actively engaged in opposing Satan in every area of culture: government, education, media, arts and entertainment, religion, family, and business.

The Great Commission

The social and governmental concerns of modern Postmillennialists are rooted in the spiritual commitments of their predecessors. Postmillennialists have always had a very optimistic view of Jesus's Great Commission in Matthew 28:18–20: "All authority in heaven and on earth has been given to me. Go therefore and make disciples of all nations, baptizing them in the name of the Father and of the Son and of the Holy Spirit, teaching them to observe all that I have commanded you. And behold, I am with you always, to the end of the age."

Because of Jesus's declaration of universal authority and the power of the Holy Spirit, Postmillennialists believe his goal far exceeds merely preaching the gospel to all nations. In their view, not only do all nations on earth hear the gospel, but most of the people on earth will eventually become Jesus's disciples.[10] Of course, the Great Commission made great progress in the first century and has been expanding ever since. But Postmillennialists believe at some point in the future it will reach its zenith, and the millennium will reach its prophesied magnitude of influence.

Ken Gentry writes,

> The Lord of lords amply equips his church for the task of world evangelistic success. Among the abundant divine provisions for the church are the following:
>
> (1) We have the very presence of the risen Christ with us. . . .
> (2) We are indwelt by the Holy Spirit from on high. . . .
> (3) The Father delights in saving sinners. . . .
> (4) We have the gospel, which is the very "power of God" unto salvation. . . .
> (5) To undergird and empower us to gospel victory, we have full access to God in prayer through Jesus' name. . . .
> (6) Though we have supernatural opposition in Satan, he is a defeated foe as a result of the first advent of Christ.[11]

Gentry does not contend that these views mean God intends to have the entire world declare loyalty to Christ Jesus. However, he concludes that these ideas are plain and powerful enough in Scripture to give credence to a postmillennial view that trumpets Christ's eventual reign over this earthly reality.[12]

Biblical Support for Postmillennialism

While evangelistic and political concerns often seem to kindle Postmillennial perspectives, its best advocates base their views on Scripture. Postmillennialists believe there's strong biblical support for their claims of end-times optimism, especially the worldwide success of the Great Commission. They would point to the following passages that describe the remarkable spread of the gospel:

> The kingdom of heaven is like a grain of mustard seed that a man took and sowed in his field. It is the smallest of all seeds, but when it has grown *it is larger than all the garden plants and becomes a tree*, so that the birds of the air come and make nests in its branches. (Matt. 13:31–32)

> The kingdom of heaven is like leaven that a woman took and hid in three measures of flour, *till it was all leavened*. (Matt. 13:33)

> For God did not send his Son into the world to condemn the world, but *in order that the world might be saved* through him. (John 3:17)

> Now is the judgment of this world; now will the ruler of this world be cast out. And I, when I am lifted up from the earth, *will draw all people to myself*. (John 12:31–32)

> He is the propitiation for our sins, and not for ours only but also *for the sins of the whole world*. (1 John 2:2)

Ken Gentry acknowledges that these passages do not teach an "each-and-every universalism" in which all people become followers of Christ. He recognizes that there are still "weeds" in the wheatfield at the end of the parable (Matt. 13:25). Still, he understands the harvest described is meant to assure us that there will be a coming day in which the "vast majority" of humanity will be redeemed, as our world is transformed by Christ's witness and work from present chaos to Christ's future kingdom.[13]

How do Postmillennialists deal with Jesus's teaching in Matthew 7:14 that "the gate is narrow and the way is hard that leads to life, and those who find it are few"? Doesn't this indicate pretty conclusively that the majority of people will not be saved—and thus upend the optimism of the Postmillennialists?

We are usually mistaken if we think that faithful people who hold to a biblical perspective different from ours have not read their Bibles. Postmillennialists certainly know Jesus's statement about the narrow way, but they don't think it applies to salvation. Rather, they point out that Jesus's disciples were his immediate audience. So his point was to indicate to his disciples how hard it was to live consistently for him rather than to join with the crowds of the world in paths that are destructive to their fellowship with him and witness of him. This interpretation presumes that within the context of the passage Jesus is talking to his disciples about their sanctification, not their salvation.[14] He is not saying that only a few will be saved but that few will consistently avoid the destructive paths of the world. Postmillennialists, with many other faithful preachers, would say that we all need to learn to depend upon the grace of Jesus as we should for a life of daily obedience.

Postmillennialists also believe the Old Testament supports the idea of a millennial kingdom that will extend throughout the earth. They would cite the following passages that predict Christ's influence throughout all nations:

> All the ends of the earth shall remember
>   and turn to the Lord,
> and *all the families of the nations*
>   *shall worship* before you. (Ps. 22:27)
>
> May God be gracious to us and bless us
>   and make his face to shine upon us,

that your way may be known on earth,
    your saving power *among all nations*. (Ps. 67:1–2)

God shall bless us;
    let *all the ends of the earth fear him*. (Ps. 67:7)

All the nations you have made shall come
    and worship before you, O Lord,
    and shall glorify your name. (Ps. 86:9)

The LORD says to my Lord:
    "Sit at my right hand,
until *I make your enemies your footstool*." (Ps. 110:1)

Postmillennialists urge those who are skeptical of this perspective to consider how the apostle Peter himself interpreted the fulfillment of Psalm 110 on the day of Pentecost:

This Jesus God raised up, and of that we all are witnesses. Being therefore exalted at the right hand of God, and having received from the Father the promise of the Holy Spirit, he has poured out this that you yourselves are seeing and hearing. For David did not ascend into the heavens, but he himself says,

"The Lord said to my Lord,
'Sit at my right hand,
    until I make your enemies your footstool.'"

Let all the house of Israel therefore know for certain that God has made him both Lord and Christ, this Jesus whom you crucified. (Acts 2:32–36)

Obviously, Peter and the other apostles believed that Jesus had fulfilled the prophetic words of Psalm 110. But Postmillennialists would also point out that Jesus, who is currently seated at the right hand of God in heaven, will remain there until he makes his enemies a footstool for his feet. They believe this will happen during the earthly millennium prior to the Lord's return.

Biblical Challenges to Postmillennialism

But what about Revelation 20, which speaks of the thousand-year reign of Christ? Do Postmillennialists believe that chapter of Scripture supports their position?

It would be fair to say that many Postmillennialists are frustrated by what they consider an overemphasis on this chapter by those with other views of the end times. Princeton theologian B. B. Warfield wrote, "Nothing, indeed, seems to have been more common in all ages of the Church than to frame an eschatological scheme from this passage, imperfectly understood, and then to impose this scheme on the rest of Scripture."[15] James L. Blevins also critiques the other views by observing that "the millennium becomes 'the tail that wags the dog.'"[16] Ken Gentry candidly acknowledges that he would prefer not to highlight the content of Revelation 20 because so many people seem to let it overshadow the teaching of clearer passages.[17] But this does not mean Postmillennialists have no explanation for this important chapter in Scripture.

Postmillennialists handle Revelation 20 by interpreting the thousand years figuratively rather than literally—and believe that Scripture gives justification for this:

> The thousand years in Revelation 20 seem to function as a symbolic value, not strictly limited to a literal thousand-year period. After all, (1) this is clearly a vision in that it opens: "and I saw" (Rev. 20:1a); (2) the perfectly rounded and exact numerical value seems more compatible with a figurative interpretation; (3) the first event in the vision is the binding of Satan with a chain, which surely is not literal.[18]

So Postmillennialists look to both the context and the language of the text to argue that it presents a symbolic view of the long-lasting kingdom of Christ that he established during his first coming—a kingdom that will eventually expand throughout the world before his return. For a Postmillennialist, the *thousand* years of Revelation 20 is no more literal than Psalm 50:10, where God declares, "Every beast of the forest is mine, the cattle on a *thousand* hills." God actually (literally) owns the cattle on many more than a thousand hills, and he will rule for more than a thousand years. That doesn't make the Scripture references inaccurate but simply indicates they are using a figure of speech to represent "a whole lot." Postmillennialists look at these "thousand" references the way that we talk about telling our kids a "million" times to shut the back door. The exact number is not the point; the significance of the number is.

What Will the Millennial Kingdom Be Like?

In order to understand the Postmillennialists' view of the millennium, you must remember that it doesn't appear abruptly in their scenarios but gradually throughout human history as more and more people become Christians. Remember, Postmillennialism is a long hill climb. According to Loraine Boettner, even today we see the fruits of Christ's expanding kingdom on earth. Writing in the late twentieth century, he said, "Today the world at large is on a far higher plane. . . . Slavery and polygamy have practically disappeared. The status of women and children has been improved immeasurably. Social and economic conditions in almost all nations have reached a new level."[19]

Boettner goes on to describe other significant strides in world improvement that he thought had been made in recent years. For example:

- The United States, which he refers to as an "enlightened and predominantly Protestant nation," has given billions of dollars for foreign aid—more than any other nation in history.

154

- The Bible is now available in whole or part to 98 percent of the people of the world.

- Christianity has grown more in the last one hundred years than in the previous eighteen hundred years.

- Through the influence of the church, numerous schools and hospitals have been founded, and social services have greatly increased.

- Our modes of transportation have changed more in the last hundred and fifty years than in the preceding two thousand.[20]

In the years since Boettner wrote, there are many more spiritual and cultural advances to celebrate: more Bible translations, more vaccines, wondrous technology, reduced poverty, reduced famine, perhaps less racism, vastly expanded communication, no world war, amazing transportation for land, sea, sky, and space—and remarkably more Christians around the world, especially in the global south. But these are only the beginning glimmers of the Postmillennial vision! Robert G. Clouse summarizes what is to come according to Postmillennialists:

> The spread of the gospel will cause the world to be Christianized and result in a long age of peace and prosperity called the millennium. . . . Evil is not eliminated but will be reduced to a minimum as the moral and spiritual influence of Christians is heightened. The church will assume greater importance and many social, economic and educational problems will be solved. This period closes with the second coming of Christ, the resurrection of the dead and the final judgement.[21]

Of course, since Boettner and Clouse wrote there have been significant challenges to their view that the world is getting better. The twentieth century ended as the world's bloodiest. The first quarter of the twenty-first century has seen the largest displacement of people in history through war, economic inequities, political upheavals, and societal corruption, chaos, or cruelty. By some accounts the twentieth century was the most dangerous for Christians worldwide, and such patterns are continuing this century through government-approved or government-organized persecutions.[22] The early twenty-first century has reexperienced pandemics that most experts thought had been overcome due to the scientific triumphs against similar ills in the early decades of the twentieth century. There seems to be little that would cause us to conclude that the moral condition of the world or of the individuals in it is improving.

Some researchers counter with evidence of spectacular advances in farming, technology, medicine, science, democratic reforms, and economic conditions that have made amazing progress against famine, poverty, disease, prejudice, intolerance, and illiteracy.[23] The condition of women, children, and workers is undeniably better than at any time in world history, and clearly improved since the time of Christ, when they had no rights to fair or moral treatment under the Roman Empire.[24] Christian missiologists will also remind us that through the perseverance and progress of the gospel, there are an estimated 2.4 billion Christians alive today, making Christianity the world's largest religion—with an estimated 65 million more people being added to this faith every year.[25]

So, should our end-times view be framed more by the world's evils and national tragedies or by gospel progress and human triumphs? Clearly, Postmillennialists would lean toward the latter. They are glass-half-full rather than glass-half-empty people. They focus much more on the progress of civilization and the church than on the hardships and suffering that also confront our modern world. There should be something in each of God's people that hopes they're right. During important periods of church history many Christians have held to this optimistic view until prolonged features of the fall have dissuaded them. If Postmillennialists are right, let's pray that we're soon coming to the end of such evil and pain.

10

Which View
Should I Believe?

In the Dr. Seuss book *Which Pet Should I Get?*, a boy and his sister go to a pet store. Their father had told them they could choose only one pet to bring home by noon. At first the boy chooses a dog, but then his sister chooses a cat. Then they see a bird and a rabbit and a fish! There are so many choices, they can't make up their minds. And Dr. Seuss adds, "You see how it is when you pick out a pet? How can you make up your mind what to get?" At the conclusion of the book, we never find out which pet they choose. Instead, the boy tells us,

> "I will do it right now. I will do it!" I said. "I will make up the mind that is up in my head." The dog . . . ? Or the rabbit . . . ? The fish . . . ? Or the cat . . . ? I picked one out fast, and then that was that.[1]

Of course, deciding which view of the end times makes the most sense is far more significant than choosing a dog or a cat—although pet lovers may tell you otherwise! And throughout this book I've tried to be as objective as I can so that you could make up your own mind. But if you still cannot decide, this chapter will offer some of the key factors you need to consider carefully.

Literal or Spiritual?

Traditional Dispensationalists have contended that they're the group that most consistently interprets Old Testament prophecy literally. Of course, the other groups discussed in this book disagree. They all understand that a fair and accurate reading requires taking the Bible in its normal or plain sense. Dr. R. C. Sproul wrote:

> The most basic rule of biblical interpretation that we can follow is that we should interpret the Bible literally. What does this mean? Essentially, we are not to treat Scripture like a secret code book; rather, we are to read the Bible as we would read any other work of literature. In other words, our goal is to read the Scriptures according to the intent of its authors and the literary conventions of the particular style that is being used. We do not read poetry the same way we read historical narrative, for example, for we know that poetry employs rich imagery that often serves as a figurative depiction of reality. Historical narrative, on the other hand, tends to give us the bare facts, as it were, the orderly account of what exactly happened. In reading the Bible literally, our goal is to get at the plain sense of the text.[2]

There are many excellent books that can hone your skills for interpreting the Bible according to its plain sense. The *Gospel Transformation Study Bible* will help you see how the gospel unfolds in all of Scripture.[3] *Living By the Book* is a very helpful and accessible guide by well-known Dispensational authors.[4] One of the best books accepted by many Bible-believing students of Scripture is *How to Read the Bible for All Its Worth* by Gordon Fee and Douglas Stuart.[5] Fee and Stuart teach readers how to pick a good translation, how to understand Old Testament narrative, and how to approach the New Testament epistles and the many other genres of Scripture, including Gospels, parables, psalms, prophets, and wisdom literature. There's even a chapter on one of the most difficult books of the Bible—Revelation.

As you're deciding which approach to end-times prophecies you will follow, the most important factor to consider is what you believe is fair to the original author's intention, the Lord's eternal purpose, and other believers' understanding. As mentioned in chapter 4, the advocates of all the views in this book believe theirs is based in a literal interpretation of the Bible. By "literal" we all mean the interpretation that's most true to the literary intention of the author. It really isn't fair to say that any of these major views don't intend to honor this kind of literal interpretation or are simply spiritualizing the original text.

All the views acknowledge that there are figures, symbols, metaphors, and signs used by biblical authors. What distinguishes a classical Dispensational view isn't a rejection of all symbolism in Scripture but a rejection of the idea that the words or symbols of Old Testament prophets reference the New Testament church. The particular inconsistency that most concerns Dispensationalists is taking words specifically addressed to God's chosen people in the Old Testament era and applying them to other people who become part of the church in the New Testament age.

This isn't a difference about what a figure of speech means but about what persons are being addressed or referenced in the Old Testament. If you think that the Old Testament prophets didn't foresee the New Testament church or that God didn't intend for their words to apply to his plans to expand his covenant love to all people, then you probably will like the classical Dispensational view best. If you think that God intended for his prophets to prepare his chosen people to represent and extend his love to all people groups, then you likely will appreciate one of the other views.

Interpreting Old Testament Promises and Prophecy

You may also recall from chapter 4 that Floyd Hamilton, an Amillennialist, confessed that if he and other non-Premillennialists consistently applied the literal understanding of the Dispensational approach, the Amillennialists would have to adopt a premillennial view of the last days.[6]

Dispensationalists are on strong ground when they claim that the Jewish prophets were addressing Jewish people when they made messianic promises in the Old Testament. Thus, it's quite reasonable, if we consider authorial intent and the understanding of the original audience, to interpret those prophecies as applying only to Jews. How can anyone think differently without twisting the Bible to mean whatever we want?

The answer of non-Dispensationalists is that we cannot and must not overlook how New Testament authors treat Old Testament promises and prophecies. They certainly don't always view them literally. Let's remember the discussion from chapter 6. We saw there how Hosea 11:1 states, "When Israel was a child, I loved him, and out of Egypt I called my son," referring to when God saved Israel out of slavery in Egypt. However, when Matthew describes how Jesus's parents fled to Egypt to protect their son and then returned to Israel after the death of Herod, the apostle indicates this is a fulfillment of Hosea's words. Matthew concludes his narrative of these events by saying, "This was to fulfill what the Lord had spoken by the prophet, 'Out of Egypt I called my son'" (Matt. 2:15).

Clearly, Matthew knew that Hosea was speaking of the nation of Israel at the time of the exodus, not about Jesus at the time of his nativity. Still, Matthew understood that Jesus embodied the true Israel just as he claimed in John 15:1, saying, "I am the true vine." Also, as discussed in chapter 6, Matthew understood that this rescue trip to Egypt echoed Old Testament patterns of God's rescue of the nation of Israel, which he had called "my son" (Exod.

4:23). Matthew isn't spiritualizing the Old Testament prophecy but rather is speaking plainly to a Jewish audience who would have understood the context of his words to reveal how God was again preparing his people for rescue.

At some point in determining which millennial perspective is most helpful, you'll need to decide how to balance Old Testament promises and prophecies in their original context with their New Testament fulfillment. If you lean toward limiting meaning to what the original writers and readers could have understood, then you'll find a Dispensational reading more convincing (cf. Matt. 13:17). However, if you think that the Holy Spirit's intention was also to prepare future readers of Scripture to understand the fuller dimensions of his plans, then you'll lean toward interpretations based on the belief that the Holy Spirit enabled human writers to describe more than they understood (cf. 1 Pet. 1:12). Such a leaning shouldn't lead to fanciful interpretations with no basis in Scripture but requires believing that the divine author's full meaning becomes apparent by analyzing the dimensions of the gospel as they unfold in the New Testament.

The Historic Premillennialist scholar J. Barton Payne taught that the nearest, adequate fulfillment of a biblical prophecy is most likely what God intended to reveal through that prophecy.[7] However, determining what is an *adequate* fulfillment of a millennial promise expressed in apocalyptic language for matters such as the absence of want, conflict, or sin will challenge us until we're with the Lord in glory. If you agree with the perspective that the human author's understanding establishes the limits for what is adequate fulfillment, then you'll lean toward a Dispensational understanding. If you think the Holy Spirit could have intended for the most adequate fulfillment of inspired words to go beyond the human author's understanding, then a non-Dispensational understanding may seem more fitting.

In reality, all millennial views will expect biblical prophecy to include some symbolism and some direct reference to specific future events. How modern readers determine the intended fulfillment is often more a consequence of their overarching biblical view than the specifics of an individual text (see chap. 3). Some will base their interpretation on the presumption that God has different plans for Israel and the church. Others will read with the expectation that all Scripture is a unified message of God's unfolding plan to engraft all his people into his covenant of grace.

Both views are held by Bible-believing people seeking to be faithful to God's Word by interpreting each text as literally as they believe it was intended.[8] We don't serve God's interests by assuming those who differ with us in these perspectives are less holy or less intelligent. Instead, we should realize that all seeking to be faithful to God's Word will read as Bernard Ramm instructed when Cold War concerns made these issues the most controversial among Christians in the twentieth century: "Interpret prophecy literally unless the evidence is such that a spiritual interpretation is mandatory, e.g., where the passage is poetic, or symbolic, or apocalyptic in literary form, or where the NT evidence demands a spiritual interpretation."[9]

Understanding Daniel 9

A key example of how such an approach requires a certain amount of both humility and conviction relates to our interpretation of Daniel 9. The passage is crucial for determining whether various Old Testament prophecies apply to the time before, during, or after the millennium.

Among evangelical interpreters, there's a partial consensus about the seventy "sevens" in verses 24–27 of Daniel's prophecy (see discussion in chap. 4). Most would agree that the sevens are groups (weeks) of years and that the seventy sevens refers to a period of 490 years—whether literal or symbolic. Most interpreters would also conclude on the basis of verse 24 that during this 490-year period at least six events will happen: "(1) the finishing of transgression, (2) an end of sin, (3) an atonement of the wicked, (4) the bringing in of everlasting righteousness, (5) the sealing of vision and prophecy, and (6) an anointing of the most holy."[10] In other words, this prophecy in Daniel 9 leads up to the end of history as we know it and the beginning of the eternal state of heaven's blessings. Many would also agree that the events of Christ's ministry on earth, including his atoning death and the resurrection that ended the dominion of Satan, conclude the sixty-ninth week.[11]

But what about the gap between the sixty-ninth and seventieth weeks? Dispensational Premillennialists not only view this as the church age but also claim that God's program with Israel stopped and won't resume until the church is removed from earth through the secret rapture. They reach this conclusion on the basis of the predictions in verses 26 and 27 but would quickly admit that these two items aren't established by the clear wording of these verses. In fact, the wording in these verses is some of the most difficult and puzzling in the entire Old Testament. So interpreting Daniel 9:26–27 as prophesying a church age that excludes Israel is based not so much on the specifics of Daniel 9 but rather on Dispensational theology as a whole. Dispensational distinctives can fit into Daniel 9:26–27, but readers wouldn't have much certainty about these conclusions without a framework that requires it. This text clearly does not deny Dispensational views, but neither does it prove them by itself.

Those who aren't Dispensational Premillennialists would take a different approach. They would note that the Old Testament prophets didn't write as though there was going to be a gap between Christ's first coming and final victory. The prophets presented the coming of the Messiah as an event that would inaugurate his victorious rule without many stages between his return and his reign. Non-Dispensationalists say the stages we now perceive to be separated by many centuries were foreshortened (or telescoped) by the prophets into a unified sequence of events because of their distance from the events being prophesied—as the peaks on a mountain range look close together when viewed from a distance.[12] This unified perspective doesn't require (or allow) us to presume that the prophets didn't include the church in their foreshortened perspective.

So non-Dispensational interpreters do not think Daniel is indicating a gap between the sixty-ninth and seventieth weeks prophesied by Gabriel for Christ's ministry. They would say that any supposed gap between the weeks—which becomes thousands of years of parenthesis in the Dispensational view—would actually have to be longer than the full time period that Daniel's weeks describe. This would make the gap that Daniel does *not* mention more substantial than the periods of time he *does* describe.

Non-Dispensationalists don't agree with assigning so much history to a gap that isn't specified by Daniel. Instead, they say that the distinctions between the sets of weeks indicate successive stages in the completion of Christ's rule rather than an unforeseen gap in God's plan. For them, the weeks are about a sequence of events—including the rebuilding of Jerusalem, the defilement of the temple, the atoning work of Christ, and the destruction of Jerusalem—that must occur before Christ's final victory.[13] They don't think the gap that Dispensationalists place between the sixty-ninth and seventieth weeks of Daniel 9 is intended or necessary. As a consequence, non-Dispensational interpreters would not agree that these puzzling verses can be used to argue for an unforeseen church age, a secret rapture of the church, or separate programs of salvation for Israel and the church.

These different views of Daniel 9:26–27 have serious consequences for prophetic interpretation. Depending on which of these two perspectives you accept—an unstated gap of thousands of years or a seamless succession of events over thousands of years—aspects of the final verses of Daniel 9 could be mostly past or mostly future, the "prince" mentioned could be Jesus or the antichrist, the temple mentioned will be rebuilt in the future or is gone forever, tribulation events are behind us or THE tribulation is ahead of us, and the millennium is already present or is yet to come. I don't mention these differing conclusions to pretend that I can resolve all the mysteries. Nor do I want to cause consternation that would make readers give up on valuing the Bible's prophecies. I'm suggesting that some humility and charity are in order when considering difficult passages.

Not all passages are so puzzling. The basic message of Scripture is beyond doubt: Jesus is coming again to judge the wicked and to bless those who have placed their faith in him with eternal peace and righteousness. Whatever view you take of the events that lead to that culmination, you'll be more confident of your Savior's plan and your understanding of how it unfolds when you're courageously firm about what's clear in Scripture and graciously tentative about what will only be known when Christ appears. We should respect the humble wisdom of the great Bible scholars of other ages who tell us that it's part of the character of Scripture prophecies not to be framed so as to be understood fully before the event. Like the parables of Jesus, the intention of prophecies is to hide some things and disclose other things lest we become proud or passive in our knowledge of God's intentions.[14]

Interpreting Revelation 19–20

The kingdom of God is mentioned throughout the Bible. At certain times Jesus taught that the kingdom had already come during his earthly ministry (Matt. 11:12; 12:28; Luke 10:9–10; 11:20). At other times he said the kingdom would come soon (Mark 1:15; 9:1–2). And at still other times he seemed to indicate it would be in the distant future (Matt. 24:30–31; Luke 19:11–12). Sometimes the Bible characterizes Christ's kingdom as his physical domination of earthly powers (1 Thess. 5:1–5; Rev. 1:7; 19:20–21), and at other times it seems to indicate more of a spiritual reality (Luke 17:20–21).

The various descriptions aren't meant to confuse us but rather to help us understand the mystery that the kingdom is present whenever Christ's power dominates the evil that is in us or around us (Matt. 13:11). There is an "already" aspect of Christ's kingdom in the heart of every believer whose sin has been conquered by the grace of Jesus and whose circumstances are under the control of Jesus. Still, there's a "not yet" aspect of the kingdom that will be fully revealed when Christ physically appears again in power and great glory to destroy the influence of Satan and his allies completely (Matt. 24:30). From this perspective the fulfillment of Old Testament prophecies about the kingdom of God has already come, but the full realization and completion of Christ's kingdom isn't yet here.

We need this understanding of the mystery of Christ's kingdom to deal with prophecies that concern specific aspects of his future victory. For example, Daniel prophesies,

> In my vision at night I looked, and there before me was one like a son of man, coming with the clouds of heaven. He approached the Ancient of Days and was led into his presence. He was given authority, glory, and sovereign power; all nations and peoples of every language worshiped him. His dominion is an everlasting dominion that will not pass away, and his kingdom is one that will never be destroyed. (Dan. 7:13–14)

Just before his crucifixion, during his trial before the Sanhedrin, Jesus proclaimed that the promises in this passage refer to him (Matt. 26:64). He said that he would come to establish his kingdom on earth. But what kingdom is he referencing—the already kingdom, the not-yet kingdom of Satan's everlasting defeat, or the kingdom of a literal thousand years that Dispensationalists and Historic Premillennialists believe follows Christ's final return before Satan's final judgment?

The thousand-year reign of Christ on earth, which we call the millennium, is only mentioned in Revelation 20. Yet the timing of that millennium affects every view of the end times and, as we saw in earlier chapters, hinges on whether Revelation 19 and 20 are sequential, or whether chapter 19 ends one summary and chapter 20 begins another. So at some point those who are unsure about which view makes the most sense must roll up their sleeves and try to understand these two chapters in Revelation. There are numerous commentaries available to help you with that task, but your own sense of the weight of Scripture's material will determine your ultimate conclusions.

If the millennium references a thousand-year reign of Christ and his followers on earth prior to Satan's final overthrow, then those with a Dispensational perspective will need to be comfortable with

> two raptures—a secret rapture and a final rapture;
>
> two returns of Christ—the secret return and the final return;
>
> two kingdoms of Christ—the thousand-year millennium on this earth and the everlasting kingdom of the new heaven and new earth;
>
> three resurrections—one for believers at the secret return of Christ, a second after the final return for believers who died during the tribulation and millennium, and a third for the wicked at the last judgment;
>
> three conquests of Satan—one at the cross, one at Armageddon, and one after he is released from his millennial chains;
>
> and possibly three eternal destinies—one for unbelievers, one for believing gentiles, and one for believing Jews.

Those who have a Historic Premillennial perspective will hold to some of these same conclusions, minus the secret rapture events and separate destinies for Israel and the church.

Many New Testament scholars are uncomfortable with this doubling and tripling up of so many end-times events that seem to be single features of Christ's victory in most Scripture references (e.g., Matt. 25:31; 1 Cor. 15:20–25; 2 Tim. 4:8; Heb. 9:28; 12:26–27; 1 Pet. 1:21). These non-Dispensational interpreters would largely agree that—apart from Revelation 19 and 20—the sequence of events at the end of history would be as follows:

1. The second coming of Christ
2. The resurrection of the dead (and the transformation of living believers)
3. The final judgment
4. The creation of the new heaven and new earth
5. The eternal state

But that more streamlined sequence disregards what for many is a plain reading of the natural and chronological flow of the final chapters of Revelation. There's nothing obvious between Revelation 19 and 20 that suggests the end of one end-times summary and the beginning of another. To the contrary, chapter 19 ends with Christ's conquest and chapter 20 begins with a "then" (as in "then this happens . . .") that describes the destruction of those who have been conquered. The most natural reading seems to be a chronological one.

Those who are Premillennialists say that the end-times timeline for the rest of the New Testament must be controlled by this plain and literal reading of Revelation 19–20. In contrast, those who aren't Premillennialists say that interpretation of Revelation 19–20 should be made consistent with what is more plain in the rest of the New Testament. They'll argue that clearer passages should determine what less clear passages mean, and that more pervasive perspectives should outweigh a single text. You'll need to decide which perspective makes the most sense to you.

Is There a Future for Israel?

Often what hinders us from trying to determine which view makes the most sense isn't merely the complexity of the biblical perspectives but our familiarity with certain aspects of them. If trusted persons have taught us a view asserting that the secret rapture is certain or that it is silly, that Russia or a Middle Eastern coalition will be the aggressor of Armageddon, or that Jews will be converted en masse during the millennium, then it's hard to question that view without wondering if we're questioning Scripture. No issue puts more leverage on our hearts than whether our millennial view encourages support of Israel.

Trusted Bible teachers have variously taught that Israel must be converted prior to Christ's return or that Israel must be protected for its millennial conversion or that we must ensure the temple will be rebuilt in order to restore the sacrificial system that saves Jews or any number of other specifics that require special consideration for Israel. As mentioned earlier in this book, such considerations have long motivated political policies that have committed billions of dollars in military and missionary aid to Israel.

So when deciding which of the views in this book is most compelling, a key question must be asked: Is there a future for the nation of Israel? A Dispensational Premillennialist would answer with a firm YES! As mentioned in chapter 4, Dispensationalists believe God has two separate programs for Israel and the church, and the two should never be confused. During the church age, God is gathering both Jews and gentiles into his family, but together they constitute the church, not the nation of Israel. However, in the future millennial kingdom, God will fulfill his Old Testament promises to national Israel.

Progressive Dispensationalists would also answer yes when asked whether God has a future plan for Israel, but with an important twist. They believe there's only one spiritual family in Christ—the church. But they point out that the church is made up of people of all nations. As John tells us in Revelation 7:9, "After this I looked, and behold, a great multitude that no one could number, from every nation, from all tribes and peoples and languages, standing before the throne and before the Lamb." Since people from all nations will be included in the eternal kingdom, Progressive Dispensationalists reason that God can still fulfill his promises to national, ethnic, territorial Israel by including them in the church.

In fact, Progressive Dispensationalists join with many Historic Premillennialists in believing that God intends to bring many Jews to faith in Christ. They believe this is the explicit point being made by the apostle Paul when he describes God's "irrevocable" promises in Romans 9 and 11. Though Historic Premillennialists have more commitment to ethnic Jews than to the political entity that identifies as national Israel, both classical and Progressive Dispensationalists tend to believe there will be a *restoration* of national Israel.

Some Amillennialists join with Historic Premillennialists in believing there will be a future *salvation* for the people of Israel, but they universally question whether there will be a *restoration* of national Israel as God's chosen people separate from the church. As mentioned in previous chapters, groups often base their understanding of large-scale Jewish conversion on Paul's teachings in Romans 11:

> I do not want you to be unaware of this mystery, brothers: a partial hardening has come upon Israel, until the fullness of the Gentiles has come in. And in this way all Israel will be saved, as it is written,

> "The Deliverer will come from Zion,
>   he will banish ungodliness from Jacob";
> "and this will be my covenant with them
>   when I take away their sins." (vv. 25–27)

Paul's words convince many Historic Premillennialists, with some Amillennialists and Postmillennialists, to join with Dispensationalists in looking forward to a time when the people of ethnic Israel will experience a great revival, realizing that Jesus is their promised Messiah. They'll become members of Christ's church and receive all the blessings of God's people in whatever nation they live in. This view would also affirm what Paul says in Romans 11:24, "If you [gentiles] were cut from what is by nature a wild olive tree, and grafted, contrary to nature, into a cultivated olive tree [believing Israel], how much more will these, the natural branches [unbelieving Israelites], be grafted back into their own olive tree." In other words, believing Jews will be regrafted with believing gentiles into the vine God planted to bear the hope of salvation through Jesus Christ.

We also need to acknowledge that there are other Amillennialists, Historic Premillennialists, and Postmillennialists who believe in what has been labeled (not always charitably) "replacement theology." Dr. Kenneth Gentry represents this view by writing, "We believe that the international Church has superseded for all times national Israel as the institution for the administration of divine blessing to the world." He goes on to say,

> As such, the multi-racial, international Church of Jesus Christ supersedes racial, national Israel as the focus of the kingdom of God. Indeed, we believe that the Church becomes "the Israel of God" (Gal. 6:16), the "seed of Abraham" (Gal. 3:29), "the circumcision" (Phil. 3:3), the "temple of God" (Eph. 2:19–22), and so forth. We believe that Jew and Gentile are eternally merged into a "new man" in the Church of Jesus Christ (Eph. 2:12–18). What God hath joined together let no man put asunder![15]

So we can see that each of the millennial views answers the question "Is there a future for Israel?" in different ways. Some expect there will be both a restoration of ethnic Israel and a future revival among the Jewish people, who will come to Christ in unprecedented numbers. Others claim there will be a revival among the Jewish people but not necessarily a restoration of faith for national Israel. Finally, some believe that the church has totally replaced Israel as God's chosen people and that Israel, as a special group, no longer has a distinct role in God's plan of redemption. You will need to decide which view has the best biblical support.

It Will All Work Out in the End

Some readers will view this chapter as an opportunity to consider how their view compares to others' perspectives on the end times. Perhaps my words have helped to explain what others believe or even to clarify what convictions you have and why you have them. If you're in that category, I pray that you will enjoy considering how God is encouraging you with the assurance that the future is in his hands. In the end, we all agree God wins and we are his forever. Even where there are differences in perspective about the end times, there is much to encourage the people of God who will unite around his Word and not make unkind or uninformed judgments about those who are doing their best to remain faithful to the basic truths all Christians affirm.

I recognize other readers may feel worn out with reading about the differences Bible teachers debate about the end times. Such readers may think it's simply not worth the effort to plow ahead and try to figure out what God wants you to believe. If that describes you, then you may find comfort in a little story that has been told many times.

Once upon a time, a man was asked whether he was a Premillennialist, an Amillennialist, or a Postmillennialist. He responded by saying he was a *Pan*-millennialist. When asked what that meant, he replied, "I believe it will all pan out in the end." Although the corny joke is old, it's absolutely true! What's more, it's an appropriate way to introduce the next two chapters in which I stop spelling out our differences and joyfully declare the hope that all Christians share about the end times.

The old joke that "it will all pan out in the end" shouldn't be allowed to diminish in the slightest the conviction that Jesus is coming again. Lack of certainty about millennial views isn't lack of certainty about essential gospel truths. The Savior who gave himself to save us from our sins will return for those who have trusted him to pardon them. He will rescue these from the evil of this world. He will judge the living and the dead, assigning the rebellious to everlasting punishment and reigning with those made righteous by his blood in an eternal kingdom that perfectly reflects his character and care for all who have ever loved him. There will be no sin or its consequences in that place of new heaven and new earth. God's beloved from all ages will be reunited and made whole in body and pure in spirit for a world made perfect for his glory and by his power, forever living in the light and love of the Lamb.

The Hope
All Christians Share, Part 1

Essentials for Eternity

The Center for the Study of Global Christianity at Gordon-Conwell Theological Seminary estimates that there are currently 45,000 Protestant denominations.[1] Some of these formed because of doctrinal differences. Others desired a specific form of church government. Still others promoted a certain form of baptism or focused on the gifts of the Holy Spirit or held a particular view of God's sovereignty. Whatever the reason, the multiplication of so many denominations seems a far cry from Jesus's words in John 17:20–21: "I pray also for those who will believe in me through their message, that all of them may

Beliefs That Unify

be one, Father, just as you are in me and I am in you. May they also be in us so that the world may believe that you have sent me" (NIV).

Thus far, this book has focused on different views of the end times—especially how they consider the millennial kingdom. But we need to remember that people aren't saved from hell and secured for heaven because they have a correct view of the millennium. No one ceases to be our brother or sister in Christ simply because they have a different millennial view. We're only saved from the consequences of our sin through faith in the grace of God that's provided by the perfect life, sacrificial death, and resurrection victory of Jesus Christ. Millennial views describe the sequences and dimensions of the future hope our Savior provides, but they don't qualify us for that hope if we're right or disqualify us from heaven if we're wrong.

How important are millennial differences in light of the essential beliefs of the Christian faith? Craig Blomberg provides a valuable perspective on this issue:

> In my ideal theological world, there would be no church or para-church organization, including seminaries, that would make a certain belief about the millennium or the tribulation a requirement of anything, such as membership, employment, or the like. If we believe in the literal, visible, public return of Christ to usher in the judgment of the living and the dead, if we believe in the bodily resurrection of all people, some to eternal life and others to eternal destruction, surely we can agree to disagree in love over the particulars on which intelligent, godly, Bible-believing Christians have never achieved consensus and yet fellowship and work together at every level of Christian service and activity. The classic orthodox creeds of the patristic period, like the major confessions of faith from the Protestant Reformation, never required more than this.[2]

Whatever view you hold about the millennium or the sequence of the end times, rejoice that there are core beliefs that all Christians hold in common. This chapter will remind us of these shared core beliefs. But this chapter and the next will also provide another cause for rejoicing: a reminder of the aspects of our end-times hope that all Christians share. Despite our differing millennial views, the dearest and most important features that the Bible reveals about the end times are clear enough to unite us in endurance for earth's trials, comfort for life's tragedies, and faith for eternity's blessings. These beliefs that constitute our shared hope are the blessings of this chapter and the bonds of our eternity.

We Agree the Bible Is the Word of God

Most of those reading this book believe that the Bible is the Word of God. To be more specific, although the Bible was written by mere humans, we believe they were inspired by the Holy Spirit to write only what God intended to say. This is especially important to note for prophecies that test our imaginations and even our credulity. That is why the apostle Peter is careful to assure us, "No prophecy of Scripture comes from someone's own interpretation. For no prophecy was ever produced by the will of man, but men spoke from God as they were carried along by the Holy Spirit" (2 Pet. 1:20–21).

The prophecies of Scripture aren't the only portions provided by God's supernatural care. The apostle Paul says, "All Scripture is breathed out by God and profitable for teaching, for reproof, for correction, and for training in righteousness" (2 Tim. 3:16). Because our God is the ultimate author of all Scripture, the sixty-six books of the Bible, though written by different authors across many lands and centuries, contain one unified story of God's gracious plan to bless his people. The story begins with creation, then records the sad fall of humanity, continues with God's resolute plan of redemption that culminates in the ministry of Jesus Christ, and concludes with the consummation of all

God's plans and promises in the perfections of the new heaven and new earth.

We not only believe there's a fundamental unity in the biblical record that helps us understand how its various books and portions relate to one another and to God's larger redemptive plan; we also believe that the Holy Spirit inspired Scripture to guard it from the limitations of other books. Writers inspired by the Holy Spirit can accurately describe events yet to come because our God knows the end from the beginning (Isa. 46:9–10).

God's knowledge affects the content of the Bible, and so does his character. Faithful Christians often describe the Bible as *inerrant*, meaning that the Bible teaches truth without error. Others prefer the word *infallible*, claiming that the Bible cannot teach anything that isn't true—just as it is impossible for God to lie (Heb. 6:18). Either way, all evangelical Christians believe that the Bible is true and trustworthy in everything that it affirms because that's the nature of the God who inspired its contents. The psalmist describes the features of God's Word as "perfect," "sure," "right," "pure," "clean," "true," and "righteous altogether" because such is the character of the God who inspired the whole (Ps. 19:7–9). God's product necessarily reflects his nature.

Because God's Word reflects his nature and purposes, we believe that we should interpret the Bible as he intended. The literary forms and conventions God inspired the human authors to use need to be studied to understand what the Holy Spirit intended to convey. This means that we believe the Bible should be interpreted literally—that is, in its *literary* sense. We are not to interpret Scripture by free association of its words with our culture or our imagination.

We look at the grammatical and historical context of the human writers to determine what they meant with their words. As explained earlier in this book, our goal is to read every text of Scripture in context and according to the intent of its authors with consideration of the language and literary conventions of the age and the particular style each author used. This approach requires us to remember that authors of the Bible wrote in a variety of literary styles or genres, such as historical narrative, poetry, proverbs, gospels, parables, and letters. As a result, when we read in Psalm 91:4 that God "will cover you with his pinions, and under his wings you will find refuge," we know the author isn't saying that God is a bird! The psalmist is using a metaphor. In the same way, when Paul tells us in 1 Corinthians 15:4–5 that Jesus "was raised on the third day in accordance with the Scriptures, and that he appeared to Cephas, then to the twelve," we conclude that he's speaking of historical events because he's giving the testimony of eyewitnesses.

When it comes to interpreting prophecies, we must acknowledge that we're frequently dealing with apocalyptic (i.e., divine revelation) language that's rich in symbolism, imagery, and wording that stretches the capacities of human expression to capture the realities of spiritual warfare, earth's destruction, heaven's glories, and hell's horrors. We believe such expressions are no less true, but neither are they as easily interpreted as other portions of Scripture. Our faith in the truth of Scripture should keep us sure of heaven. Scripture's testimony of heaven's magnificence should keep us humble about our understanding of all the dimensions of its aspects or arrival.

We Agree That Jesus Died on the Cross for Our Sins

If our salvation doesn't depend on our view of the rapture, the timing of the tribulation, or how we interpret Revelation 20, then what is the basis of our eternal relationship with God? Most people reading this book will agree that we're saved by grace through faith in Jesus's atoning death and victorious resurrection over the power of sin: "For by grace you have been saved through faith. And this is not your own doing; it is the gift of God, not a result of works, so that no one may boast" (Eph. 2:8–9).

178

Why Christ died can be explained from a variety of perspectives. The moral influence theory teaches that Jesus died as a moral example to inspire humanity to follow in his selfless steps. The *Christus Victor* view claims that Jesus died to lead our conquest over the powers of evil—not only sin and death but also the world's corruptions and the devil's schemes. The satisfaction theory says that Jesus Christ died either to purchase us from Satan's clutches or to pay back God for the trouble caused by human sin.[3]

Each of these views contains an element of truth. But those reading this book probably realize that Jesus's death accomplished something much deeper and more profound than giving us a good moral example that we cannot perfectly follow or crushing Satan's influence for limited times in limited places or paying off God (or Satan) for our souls. The view that gives our souls the greatest hope and has the most support in Scripture identifies Jesus as a penal substitutionary atonement, a perfect sacrifice that God provided to satisfy divine justice by putting the penalty for our sin on him. This view can be described as follows:

> Jesus Christ died to satisfy God's wrath against human sin. Jesus was punished (penal) in the place of sinners (substitution) in order to satisfy the justice of God and the legal demand of God to punish sin. In the light of Jesus' death, God can now forgive the sinner because Jesus Christ was punished in the place of the sinner, in this way meeting the retributive requirements of God's justice.[4]

We claim the eternal blessings of this provision by believing that Christ's gracious substitution, rather than any merit in us, is the basis for our salvation from sin and death.

We Agree Jesus Rose from the Dead

Every true Christian believes not only that Jesus died on the cross but also that he was raised from the dead. Paul tells the Corinthians,

"In fact Christ has been raised from the dead, the firstfruits of those who have fallen asleep. For as by a man came death, by a man has come also the resurrection of the dead. For as in Adam all die, so also in Christ shall all be made alive" (1 Cor. 15:20–22).

The apostles gave their lives to testify to the fact that Jesus rose again—not only in the teachings of his followers or in the activities of the church but physically and really. Life came back into the mortal body that had been cruelly killed on the cross, and Jesus walked again on this earth before he ascended to heaven as our Lord (Acts 1:6–11). There he now intercedes for us at God's right hand (Rom. 8:34) and works all things together for our good (Rom. 8:28).

Christ's resurrection was witnessed by many people, not just those in Jesus's inner circle. The apostle Paul writes,

> For I delivered to you as of first importance what I also received: that Christ died for our sins in accordance with the Scriptures, that he was buried, that he was raised on the third day in accordance with the Scriptures, and that he appeared to Cephas, then to the twelve. Then he appeared to more than five hundred brothers at one time, most of whom are still alive, though some have fallen asleep. Then he appeared to James, then to all the apostles. Last of all, as to one untimely born, he appeared also to me. (1 Cor. 15:3–8)

Why are the apostles so insistent that Jesus physically rose from the dead? Jesus's resurrection accomplished far more than giving him a body to return to heaven. The same body that died on the cross was brought back to life by God himself. This was the evidence that the power of sin, which had reigned since Adam brought death into the world, was broken and all who united themselves to Christ by faith would ultimately experience the same victory over death.

Not only will our souls go to heaven when we die, but when Jesus returns to earth our bodies will be made like his (1 John 3:2).

Jesus's resurrected body was immortal and indestructible—just as ours will be when he returns! The imperfections caused by age, disease, and our habits will be removed. Again Paul writes, "I tell you this, brothers: flesh and blood cannot inherit the kingdom of God, nor does the perishable inherit the imperishable. . . . For this perishable body must put on the imperishable, and this mortal body must put on immortality" (1 Cor. 15:50, 53).

We Agree the Holy Spirit Indwells All True Believers

Every Christian has received the gift of the Holy Spirit. Before Jesus went to the cross, he promised that he wouldn't leave his followers alone. He told his disciples, "I will not leave you as orphans; I will come to you" (John 14:18). He spoke not only about his resurrection from the dead but also about the Holy Spirit: "But the Helper, the Holy Spirit, whom the Father will send in my name, he will teach you all things and bring to your remembrance all that I have said to you" (v. 26). Therefore, if you're a Christian, you have the Spirit of God living within you. The Bible teaches that this promise is true for every Christian, regardless of their view of the end times.

Before Jesus ascended into heaven, he knew that his disciples needed the power of God if they were to fulfill his command to "make disciples of all nations" (Matt. 28:19–20). So he gave them instructions not to leave Jerusalem "but to wait for the promise of the Father, which, he said, 'you heard from me; for John baptized with water, but you will be baptized with the Holy Spirit not many days from now'" (Act 1:4–5). Then, on the day of Pentecost fifty days after Jesus's resurrection, the Holy Spirit was poured out on his followers, and they immediately began declaring the wonders of God in the languages of the crowds that were present. They also proclaimed the good news about Jesus, and about three thousand people became Christians that day!

Today that same Spirit not only lives in us but also empowers the transformation in our lives that honors Christ and motivates us to share the gospel with others. Paul encouraged believers in the early church who were struggling to honor Jesus, reminding them, "Do you not know that you are God's temple and that God's Spirit dwells in you?" (1 Cor. 3:16). The apostle John tells us that we need not fear even the power of the antichrist because "he who is in you is greater than he who is in the world" (1 John 4:3–4).

There are profound implications of the Spirit of God indwelling us. First, we are assured that no outside force of evil is greater than God's power to fulfill his purposes for our lives (Rom. 8:28). Second, we are promised that internal spiritual power spares us from helplessness against our sinful inclinations. The apostle Paul assures us that sin no longer has dominion over those who put their faith in Christ (Rom. 6:6, 14). We may choose to yield to temptation, but true Christians are never again powerless against sin as we were prior to the indwelling of God's Spirit.

Some Christians consider the land where God promised to dwell with Israel and defeat their enemies as an eternal promise that will be physically fulfilled in the end times. Other Christians believe that God has already laid claim on that territory spiritually when he makes the hearts of believers his temple. What we all agree upon is that believers are indwelt by the Spirit who enables them to act faithfully in whatever land they now dwell.

The Hope
All Christians Share, Part 2

Essentials for the End Times

We Agree Suffering and Persecution Will Intensify in the Last Days

Because we live in a sinful, fallen world, everyone suffers. People throughout the world endure disease, live with war, go hungry, experience cruelty or loss, and cannot offer their children a certain future. These realities apply to both Christians and non-Christians. Until Christ returns, the corruptions of our world will affect all our lives and our loved ones. Jesus said to his followers, "In this world you will have tribulation" (many translations say "trouble," but the original Greek word is the same as "tribulation"). Then he adds, "But take heart; I have overcome the world" (John 16:33). How? Paul explains that God "comforts us in all our affliction, so that we may be able to comfort those who are in any affliction,

with the comfort with which we ourselves are comforted by God"
(2 Cor. 1:4).

What comfort do we have in this fallen world? Not the assurance of unlimited affluence or peace—though God may grant
each for a time or to a degree. Our more certain comfort is that
no trouble will last forever because we'll experience the end of
troubles either when we go to heaven or when Christ returns to
earth. And until then we are assured that "for those who love
God all things work together for good" (Rom. 8:28). This doesn't
mean that all things seem good or feel good but that all things are
working to bring about God's greatest blessings for our eternity.

Even though God is working all things together for good, a
specific type of suffering remains certain for faithful followers of
Jesus Christ. Paul tells us that "all who desire to live a godly life in
Christ Jesus will be persecuted" (2 Tim. 3:12). Throughout history,
those who faithfully represent Jesus in this world have suffered.
That suffering continues today.

The Center for the Study of Global Christianity at Gordon-
Conwell Theological Seminary estimates that there have been
over 70 million Christians martyred within the past two thousand years. Over half of these died in the twentieth century under
fascist and communist regimes, and over the ten-year period from
2000–2010 it is estimated that approximately 100,000 Christians
were martyred each year (1 million total).[1] Christians face persecution in places such as Iran, China, India, Syria, Afghanistan,
and North Korea, as well as in your hometown, in your children's
school, and in your workplace.[2] All who stand for Christ stand
against the world, and we know the world will push back. The
Holy Spirit will help us to stay faithful, but faithfulness is costly,
and that will be more and more evident as the end of the end
times approaches.

It's important for us to note that *all* the views presented in
this book agree that suffering for Christ will intensify before the
Lord returns.[3] As that day approaches, the forces of evil will grow

stronger than ever and will challenge the church. That opposition will result in conflict between God's people and the evil forces (both human and spiritual) of this world. I don't know what form that conflict will take, but I'm convinced that if God's people are living for him, they will have to stand strong and fight against the forces of darkness. That's why Jesus told his followers, "If anyone would come after me, let him deny himself and take up his cross and follow me. For whoever would save his life will lose it, but whoever loses his life for my sake will find it" (Matt. 16:24–25).

God warns us in his Word about the greater evils of the last days so that we won't lose hope when we face growing opposition and fearsome persecution. Rather, these challenges should make us watch more expectantly for God's rescue, encourage others to do the same, and stir living faithfully amid opposition and persecution in anticipation of Christ's imminent return (Heb. 10:24–25). The secularization of society, the erosion of morals, the threats against Christians, and the compromises of the church and many Christians within it shouldn't send us into despair but into greater anticipation of our Savior's nearness that generates fearless faithfulness. If we truly believe that Christ and his armies are near, then we don't want to faint or falter in our witness of the glory and grace that will soon embrace us and rout God's enemies.

We need to remember that the Bible reveals both hopeful and challenging aspects of the end times to encourage faithfulness. On this we also agree. The great Dispensational teacher and preacher J. Dwight Pentecost once wrote,

> A short time ago, I took occasion to go through the New Testament to mark each reference to the coming of the Lord Jesus Christ and to observe the use made of that teaching about His coming. I was struck anew with the fact that almost without exception, when the coming of Christ is mentioned in the New Testament, it is followed by an exhortation to godliness and holy living.[4]

Similarly, Amillennialist preacher David Hall writes about the purpose of the book of Revelation: "When the persecutions or difficulties came about soon, God didn't want his people disheartened. This a warning not to lose heart in the face of it [sic]."[5] Postmillennialist Loraine Boettner adds that biblical prophecies prepare us for our spiritual battles because Christ's promise to defeat evil "gives us special confidence for believing in the future progress of the Church."[6]

I cite these encouragements from authors of different perspectives to make it clear that each believes the purpose of the end-times prophecies in Scripture is to give Christians the hope they need for the trials of today.[7] At times, the debates over who has the best end-times view degenerate into unfair caricatures of certain views as optimistic and others as pessimistic. The caricatures are usually followed by accusations that the former are prone to patient passivity and the latter to misguided missionary activity.

There is, of course, a sense in which all of the views have a degree of pessimism: Premillennialists tend to think the world is getting worse until Christ returns, and Amillennialists and Postmillennialists think it will improve (except for a brief final season of evil) prior to Christ's return. But each view includes the fundamental optimism that Christ will rescue us from this present evil age.

Premillennialists certainly see lots of negative things happening before Christ returns. Still, their conviction that the gospel must be preached in all the earth before the end comes (Matt. 24:14) has led to incredible missionary and Bible translation efforts with the optimism of those who expect that Jesus will return soon. The Postmillennialists are certainly optimistic about the long-term progress of the church but may predict it so far into the future as to make Christians pessimistic about present gospel efforts. One contemporary commentator wisely observes, "The old Augustinian view . . . makes more sense . . . as an answer to the question of whether the times we live in are light or darkness, whether grace is everywhere or everything is falling apart. Both are true."[8]

The best spokespersons for all perspectives are aware of these dynamics and tend to join arms in declaring that the potential for Christ's imminent appearing should keep us all encouraged for and diligent in Christ's work until he comes. Jesus could come very soon, whether that's because the world quickly degenerates under an antichrist's influence or because the church rapidly progresses through the Holy Spirit's power.[9] Either way, we should be busy about the Lord's business to prepare for his kingdom's glory that he promises will come "soon" (Rev. 1:1; 22:6, 7, 20).

We Agree That There Is a Rapture and Second Coming of Christ

That preparation includes our anticipation of being "caught up" with the Lord in his glorious return. Regardless of what they teach about the timing of the rapture, all four views in this book believe in a rapture. That's because Bible-believing Christians affirm what the apostle Paul tells us in 1 Thessalonians 4:16–18:

> For the Lord himself will descend from heaven with a cry of command, with the voice of an archangel, and with the sound of the trumpet of God. And the dead in Christ will rise first. Then we who are alive, who are left, will be caught up together with them in the clouds to meet the Lord in the air, and so we will always be with the Lord. Therefore encourage one another with these words.

Of course, Dispensationalists are quick to specify that a secret rapture must first remove those in the church from the world prior to the tribulation in order to fulfill God's promises to Israel during the millennium. Still, all the views anticipate an event in which Christ physically returns in glory to rescue believers from great evil and suffering by drawing them to himself. Paul even urges us to encourage one another through trials and in the face of death itself with this promise of God's care through his risen, returning, and rescuing Son (1 Thess. 4:18)!

Every Christian looks forward to the second coming of Christ. We are united in the hope that he will return as our triumphant King and Savior who will destroy the forces of evil that have oppressed and persecuted his people. He will also return to establish the glories and blessings of his eternal kingdom with and through his people. Unfortunately, many Christians today have lost sight of the full implications of those aspects of Christ's second coming. They primarily think about heaven as God's future provision to keep us from dreading death too much. In fact, the promises of Christ's return, rescue, and reign are meant to enable us to live each day on this earth fully, faithfully, and joyfully. Eager anticipation is supposed to encourage earthly action. And with no fear of death, we can engage every challenge confident that our eternity is secure and the best is yet to come.

Here's what God's Word says about how the blessed hope of Christ's second coming should affect Christians:

> Let not your hearts be troubled. Believe in God; believe also in me. . . . And if I go and prepare a place for you, I will come again and will take you to myself, that where I am you may be also. . . . Truly, truly, I say to you, whoever believes in me will also do the works that I do; and greater works than these will he do, because I am going to the Father. (John 14:1, 3, 12)

> Now may the God of peace himself sanctify you completely, and may your whole spirit and soul and body be kept blameless at the coming of our Lord Jesus Christ. (1 Thess. 5:23)

> [We are] waiting for our blessed hope, the appearing of the glory of our great God and Savior Jesus Christ, who gave himself for us . . . who are zealous for good works. (Titus 2:13–14)

Christ, having been offered once to bear the sins of many, will appear a second time, not to deal with sin but to save those who are eagerly waiting for him. (Heb. 9:28)

Beyond the doorway that Christ opens for all believers at his second coming is eternal life in a kingdom absent of sin and filled with joy. C. S. Lewis describes our blessed hope in the final page of his book *The Last Battle* as the "real story" that goes on forever—a sweet reminder that the eternity we will claim beyond these last days is not fantasy or fiction or a dream of religious exaggeration.[10] Our hope is real, our pardon is real, our holiness will be real, our souls will be at rest, and our enjoyment of our Savior's love alongside all those who love him will be eternal. God promises that our best and unending days are ahead so that we have the confidence, courage, and convictions to live our best life now.

We Agree We Will Be Transformed at the Resurrection

Beyond the doorway that opens to Christ's kingdom at his second coming is a world that will be transformed by his goodness and grace, but we will be transformed too. You should know why this is part of our blessed hope. By the time we reach middle age, we begin to wonder what happened to the young, strong, beautiful body we once had. Then things rapidly go downhill from there! Many of us gain weight, lose muscle mass, and experience numerous aches and pains. And if that isn't bad enough, we eventually die and return to dust. George Bernard Shaw once quipped, "Life's ultimate statistic is the same for all people. One out of one dies." That's hard to deny.

But every Christian knows that isn't the end of the story. Paul tells us in 1 Corinthians 15:50–54,

I tell you this, brothers: flesh and blood cannot inherit the kingdom of God, nor does the perishable inherit the imperishable. Behold! I tell you a mystery. We shall not all sleep, but we shall all be changed, in a moment, in the twinkling of an eye, at the last trumpet. For the trumpet will sound, and the dead will be raised imperishable, and we shall be changed. For this perishable body must put on the imperishable, and this mortal body must put on immortality. When the perishable puts on the imperishable, and the mortal puts on immortality, then shall come to pass the saying that is written: "Death is swallowed up in victory."

We will live in the kingdom of Christ beyond the doorway of his second coming in new bodies that are immortal and imperishable! Aging, injury, sickness, sorrow, and death will be past. All such suffering will be a long-distant memory when only the first ten thousand years of heaven have passed—and ten thousand times ten thousand will be yet to come.

We shall enjoy one another in perfections that we have never known in this life. My aging brother, who loves Jesus but functions at the cognitive level of an eight-year-old, will be more whole and healthier than I have ever known him. Bodies ravaged by disease, damaged by accidents, betrayed by genetics, despised by their inhabitants, or neglected by caretakers will be wonderfully, beautifully, and gloriously made new in form and function forever.

In his wonderful message "The Weight of Glory," C. S. Lewis summarizes this aspect of our eternal hope, reminding us that those believers who strike us now as dull or even disdainful will one day be so clothed in Christ's glory that ordinary humans today, if they could witness such persons in their eternal state, would be tempted to fall down in worship of them.[11]

But radiant bodily health and longevity are only part of the story. Our character also will be transformed. The writer of Hebrews describes an assembly of those in heaven as "the spirits of the righteous made perfect" (Heb. 12:23). The apostle John also tells us, "We know that when he [Christ] appears we shall be like him, because we shall see him as he is. And everyone who thus hopes in him purifies himself as he is pure" (1 John 3:2–3).

The longer we live the Christian life, the more we realize that there's still an enormous gap between Christ's character and our own. We rejoice that our sins are forgiven even as we grieve that we still sin. This won't always be true, however. When Christ returns and invites his loved ones to his kingdom, that gap will be instantly closed forever. We will be beautiful not only on the outside but also on the inside. We will be forever purified from sin and perfected in holiness. We'll be able to love God with all our heart, soul, mind, and strength. And we'll love each other with the same selfless love that Christ displayed when he gave his life for us on the cross. Sin, disobedience, lack of faith, and our other innumerable character flaws will no longer plague us. We will become as pure, obedient, and loving as Jesus himself. What an amazing promise! What a blessed future is before us!

We Agree That God Will Judge the Living and the Dead

This blessed future isn't for everyone. Many people, including some Christians, flinch at the idea that God will judge and punish those who have rejected Christ. Why doesn't he simply forgive and forget? When we think that way, we forget that God is not only merciful but also just. God must be both to be righteous.

Consider if your family had been terribly wronged and abused by a criminal. If the trial judge simply declared, "The crime doesn't matter. The perpetrator is pardoned," we wouldn't consider the judgment just or the judge righteous. God must punish sin or his judgments are not just and he is not righteous. But remember that he satisfied the requirements of justice by allowing his perfectly righteous Son to suffer the penalty for the sins of all who will acknowledge their need of such grace.

God's love made provision for the scales of justice to be balanced so that you and I will not have to suffer the penalty for our sins if we trust that Jesus already did. That requires some humility on our part. We must confess that we're sinners in need of a Savior, and if we do that, there's sufficient mercy in God's heart for the worst of sinners.

God makes his love and mercy known through the ministry of his Son, but he also makes his justice and righteousness known by his promise to judge sin—whether at the cross or on the day of judgment. In Revelation 20, the apostle John describes that day of judgment, when God himself will hold court for those who think they have no need of Jesus's provision:

> Then I saw a great white throne and him who was seated on it. From his presence earth and sky fled away, and no place was found for them. And I saw the dead, great and small, standing before the throne, and books were opened. Then another book was opened, which is the book of life. And the dead were judged by what was written in the books, according to what they had done. And the sea gave up the dead who were in it, Death and Hades gave up the dead who were in them, and they were judged, each one of them, according to what they had done. Then Death and Hades were thrown into the lake of fire. This is the second death, the lake of fire. (Rev. 20:11–14)

God's judgment will be just and the punishment will fit the crime because those are the standards his character requires. There's no need to take ghoulish interest in the manner in which the wicked will be punished. The Bible presents various images of the misery of hell primarily to warn God's people to flee to the safety of their Savior. Still, the essential truth is that those who have refused to honor the Lord will ultimately get what they want—total, eternal separation from the requirements and blessings of his rule.

In his book *The Problem of Pain*, C. S. Lewis asserts that hell is locked from the inside.[12] What he meant, of course, is that those who end up in hell are there because they chose to be apart from God, including separating themselves from all that is good about him. Even in hell they aren't clamoring to worship God or submit to his righteousness. Their need to rule themselves and their unwillingness to honor him are so fierce and resolute that they would never return to God even if they had the choice to do so.

We Agree the Last Days Will Usher in the New Heaven and Earth

In recent years, a number of books have been written on near-death experiences, where people supposedly die and go to heaven for a brief period before coming back to their earthly bodies. Many of them give elaborate descriptions of what they saw and experienced. Surprisingly, the Bible says very little about what heaven is like before the final resurrection, other than telling us we will be with Christ, which will be "far better" than our earthly existence (Phil. 1:23).

Theologians remind us that not until Christ's final return will our souls and bodies be eternally united in a perfect existence. Until then, those who die are spiritually united to Christ in heaven, but their bodies remain in the earth. This "intermediate state" doesn't get a lot of definition in Scripture. Jesus calls it "Paradise" when he tells the thief on the cross next to him where death will immediately take him. Jesus also says that he will go there to prepare a place for his loved ones (John 14:1–3). Whatever that spiritual dimension is in which God dwells and immediately unites us to his Son when we die, we don't have a lot of description. We do know that believers will experience perfect peace in the presence of their Savior.

One theologian suggests that death may be like the switch on a radio that allows our souls to dial in to the presence of heaven that's already all around us like radio waves.[13] There's obviously some speculation there. We might wonder how Elijah got to such a heaven on a chariot of fire, but then we would also have to wonder why the chariot didn't burn (2 Kings 2:11–12). Whatever is the nature of this heavenly existence prior to the final resurrection, we'll ultimately have to settle with understanding it to be supernatural and, therefore, beyond our full earthly grasp. That may be why the Bible gives so little definition of its characteristics.

By contrast, the Bible says a great deal about the glories of the new heaven and earth, where we'll live eternally after Christ's return. That's the subject of the next chapter. For now, let's consider the many end-times matters about which we have discovered Christians share agreement, despite their different millennial views. This agreement is our shared hope, which is not a hope-against-hope optimism but a future confidence that God will surely fulfill the promises he has made to his people.

In the Bible, remembrance is faith in the past tense that believes what God has done; trust is faith in the present tense that acts on who God is; and hope is faith in the future tense that recalls and acts upon what God promises. Our shared hope is founded on the following principles and promises we believe God has declared in his Word and the future we have faith he will bring.

15 Aspects of the Hope All Christians Share

1. **The coming of Christ's kingdom.** In the Lord's Prayer, we pray that God's kingdom will come because we believe the completion of God's rule on earth through Christ is still in the future. We consider the prophecies of Scripture concerning this future kingdom to be true and vital for our conviction that our God is being faithful to his plan for his people.
2. **Literal interpretation.** We share the conviction that our understanding of the end times, including our millennial views, should be determined by the literary context, content, and nature of the original author's writing as intended by the Holy Spirit.

194

3. **Physical return.** We all believe that Jesus will physically return in power and great glory from his present station in heaven to rescue his people and establish his kingdom.

4. **Millennium.** All Bible-believing views of the millennium teach that there is a period in God's plan, prior to Christ's final return, in which his influence dominates and Satan's influence diminishes.

5. **Apostasy and tribulation.** We all believe a time of great evil, unbelief, and tribulation for Christ's people will immediately precede the physical return of Christ, but then he will come to rescue his people and restore our world.

6. **Antichrist.** We all believe that this period of great evil and tribulation will involve the appearance of an antichrist who will pose as an agent of good before generating great evil against God's people, but he will not ultimately succeed.

7. **Armageddon.** We all believe that Christ will engage in a great battle against his enemies to combat forces that oppose his rule and oppress his people. Jesus wins!

8. **Rescue and rapture.** We all believe that Jesus will come to rescue his people from this world's evil and rebellion, and that this rescue will involve "catching up" dead and living believers to be with him as he establishes his kingdom.

9. **Resurrection.** We share the belief that this mortal life is not the final estate for our souls or our bodies. Rather, those who have died in Christ shall be raised in newness of life when our Lord returns. The simple message that death does not win is the core hope of the gospel, teaching that no failure is final, no evil has victory, and no sin can destroy a life united to Christ.

10. **Imminent return.** We all believe that sufficient aspects of biblical prophecy have been fulfilled to make it possible that Jesus could come in the near future—or at any time. His Word makes it clear that we are already living "in these last days" (Heb. 1:2).

11. **A place for Jews.** We all believe that the promise of salvation by faith God made to Abraham and his descendants is available

to Jews in every era and that there are ethnic Jews who will claim that promise in Christ's eternal kingdom.

12. **Judgment of the living and the dead.** We all believe that all people will stand before the judgment seat of God to be judged according to our spiritual status. Believers will be judged on the basis of Christ's righteousness that covers their sin, and unbelievers will be judged according to their works that will condemn them before a holy God. Those who believe in Christ will enter his eternal kingdom of light, and those who do not will be cast into the outer darkness of hell.

13. **Satan and his allies defeated.** We share the belief that the judgment of God will include the completion of his Genesis 3:15 promise to crush Satan by casting him permanently into hell with those who have followed him.

14. **New heaven and earth.** We share the hope that the eternal destiny of all believers is intimate fellowship in body and spirit with our Savior in his eternal kingdom where there is no more darkness, pain, sin, or tears. There, all is made perfect in the light and love of the Lamb who was slain, who will then reign over all forever.

15. **Shared rule.** We share the hope that, in ways we cannot yet fully understand, Christ's loved ones not only will judge the angels (1 Cor. 6:3) but also will rule with our Savior over his kingdom as our union with him becomes complete and his heart fills ours (2 Tim. 2:11–12).

These many features of end-times consensus should remind us of the generous spirit and wisdom of Loraine Boettner, whose Postmillennial views were the most popular during the centuries surrounding this nation's founding but are the least common now:

It should be remembered, however, that while Post-, A-, and Premillennialists differ in regard to the manner and time of Christ's return, that is, in regard to the events that are to precede or follow his return, they agree in regard to the fact that He will return personally and visibly and in great glory. . . . Christ's return is taught so clearly and repeatedly in Scripture that there can be no question in this regard for those who accept the Bible as the word of God. They also agree that at His coming He will raise the dead, execute judgment, and eventually institute the eternal state. . . . Hence the matters on which they agree are much more important than those on which they differ.[14]

This book has well confirmed these observations, and I pray it will generate a similar spirit that encourages those who believe the Bible is true and Jesus is coming again to work in mutual love and respect for his mission in all the world.

Historical perspective makes it apparent that, in times of war and calamity, our spiritual inclinations lean toward Premillennial views, longing for rescue. In times of peace, progress, and prosperity, we lean toward Postmillennial views, looking for greater improvement and growth. Amillennialism tends to be the common ground of many believers in steady-state periods. None of these observations prove or disprove any of the millennial views but should make us appreciate the common aspects of all perspectives that give us a shared hope for the end times. Christians have shared the essentials of this hope through all periods of world history, and we should rejoice with them for the future glory that is the subject of our final chapter.

"Behold, I Am Making All Things New"

In an essay titled "But Man Fell on Earth," German scholar and preacher Helmut Thielicke talks about visiting a group of young soldiers on a World War II battlefield the day one of their friends had been killed. The boys gathered around the pastor "almost like chicks round a hen." He tried to speak words of comfort to them but felt utterly helpless. He writes,

> But then the thing happened that accounts for my relating this incident at all. On my way home the moonlight lay upon the quiet valley, the white flowers of the trees shimmered in this soft light, and an unspeakable peace and stillness rested upon the landscape. The world was "like some quiet room, where wrapt in still soft gloom, we sleep away the daylight's sorrow."
>
> I mention this, not to be romantic or to gain a sentimental effect, but rather because for me this hour was a parable of the dark threshold which, the account of the Fall says, man has crossed. Before me lay the seemingly whole and healthy world of a springtime night. But in that moment its very peace was like a stab of pain. For

I knew that the peace of nature is delusive, and that I had just spoken, encompassed by a sea of blossoms, with boys whose eyes were filled with dread even though they bravely swallowed their tears.[1]

The image is a stark and sad reminder of the sin that's corrupted our world and touches everyone and everything with suffering. No one escapes, despite the peace and beauty that may surround us with poignant but temporal blessings. Pain—whether physical, emotional, relational, or spiritual—can dominate our daily reality. Despite great joys, we can't turn off the inward voices of anxiety or anger that whisper of the uncertainties that keep everything in jeopardy. The voices greet us in the morning, nag us through the day, invade our delights, and replay in endless loops that keep us from sleep, so that we're constantly fatigued and less ready to handle the pain of the next day.

Who can stop these replays? Jesus.

Who can keep the pain from dominating every day? Jesus.

Who can keep justifiable fatigue from turning to hopeless despair? Jesus.

How? Not by denying the reality of suffering or evil but by emblazoning throughout the pages of Scripture with a trumpeting crescendo in its closing pages, "This present evil world is not your final destiny—there is a home of eternal beauty and peace prepared for you." In this chapter we'll look at what the Bible says about this new home God promises to his children—our eternal home to which the end times are a doorway.

A World of Peace

The apostle John describes this future home in Revelation 21, which begins, "Then I saw a new heaven and a new earth, for the first heaven and the first earth had passed away, and the sea was no more" (v. 1). Something new, something better, replaces the world of suffering that we know. The world John sees isn't something beyond recognition. It looks like the heaven (sky) and earth that he knows, but it also looks like this earth and heaven made new. This new and real heaven and earth will be our eternal home. We won't spend eternity sitting on clouds playing harps but living fully and joyfully with restored bodies on an earth made perfect.

John concludes his statement about the realities of this new earth with the words "the sea was no more." Why is this significant? The reason isn't to tell us that we won't need or see water anymore. John is writing in the context of what the sea meant for God's people in Scripture. That context is reflected for us when we say, "Don't make waves." The phrase means "don't do anything to cause any disruption or upset." Similarly, in the cultural context of Scripture the sea often represented chaos and instability. So a world without sea waves is symbolic of a world at peace. The Bible prophesies that the fearsome waves of the sea are nullified in our eternal home. All challenges to our peace of heart and mind will be vanquished there.

Many Bible scholars say that the very first redemptive event in the Bible is recorded already in its second verse: "The earth was without form and void, and darkness was over the face of the deep. And the Spirit of God was hovering over the face of the waters" (Gen. 1:2). From that chaotic liquid beginning, the Spirit of God brought light and land that became the ordered creation before it was corrupted by the fall of humanity. A world with no sea is the restoration of the peace of a fully ordered creation.

Later, when the children of Israel were escaping the slavery of Pharoah, it was the churning Red Sea that stood in their way. Then God rescued Israel by enabling them to cross on dry land through the midst of the sea. A world where the sea gives way has the kind of peace where people are free to flourish without any slavery to the evils of sin.

And when the stormy waves of the Sea of Galilee caused the disciples to cry out, "Jesus, don't you care about us?" he cared. From a heart of compassion Jesus commanded the wind and the waves,

"Peace! Be still!" (see Mark 4:37–41). When the waves calmed, the result was peace. A future world without sea waves is a world at peace made possible by the compassion and power of God.[2]

A World Filled with God's Presence

In Revelation 21:2–3, John goes on to say, "I saw the holy city, new Jerusalem, coming down out of heaven from God, prepared as a bride adorned for her husband. And I heard a loud voice from the throne saying, 'Behold, the dwelling place of God is with man. He will dwell with them, and they will be his people, and God himself will be with them as their God.'"

When the children of Israel passed through the sea into the wilderness—a desolate, foreboding, and empty place—God told them to build a tabernacle, a portable house for him to dwell in their midst. He hadn't physically dwelt among his people since Eden. Now the same God who had created the universe, freed Israel from Pharoah's power, and thundered on Mount Sinai, says, "I will dwell with you wherever you go" (see 2 Cor. 6:16). The tabernacle was an echo of Eden's uncorrupted beauty and blessing that displayed the grace God had made available to humanity.

The tabernacle in the wilderness not only echoed Eden but was also a foretaste of the presence of God in the promised land. When God's people left the wilderness and entered the land and established their nation, they built a permanent temple in Jerusalem. At its dedication, the holy God, whose glory even the angels couldn't look upon, came among sinful, rebellious, broken people and promised that he would dwell with them and would stay with them forever (see 1 Kings 9:3).

The tabernacle also became a foretaste of the coming One who would "tabernacle" among us and send his Spirit to dwell within us despite our sin, rebellion, and brokenness (see John 1:14). The indwelling of the Holy Spirit is God's present way of going with us wherever we go and assuring us that he will stay with us forever.

201

That's why he can say, "I will never leave you or forsake you" (cf. 1 Kings 8:57; Heb. 13:5). But there's a more precious and powerful expression of that truth in our future when all the wandering of our hearts and the corruptions and distractions of this world will be gone.

When the new Jerusalem comes down from heaven to the new world God will create, then heaven and earth will be joined forever. We'll experience the full impact and blessing of his words, "I will never leave you or forsake you." We'll be with Jesus every moment of eternity in every dimension of our existence, and there will be nothing of the world's brokenness or sin between us. His heart will be for us, his everlasting arms will support us, and his joy will envelop us.

We don't now have the words or minds to capture fully the glory and goodness of our days in that land where his divine love dwells and evil cannot. But this we know: We'll live forever in the peace and presence of God. The pain and corruptions of this present existence will be banished forever. And there won't be a single second in those endless days that we don't know the perfect happiness of being fully united with Jesus and those who love him.

A World without Pain, Suffering, or Sorrow

Looking forward to our glorious future, John writes in Revelation 21:4, "He will wipe away every tear from their eyes, and death shall be no more, neither shall there be mourning, nor crying, nor pain anymore, for the former things have passed away."

Contemporary songs try to capture the peace and beauty of such a world, assuring us of an end to darkness, pain, tears, and fears. But the reality will be more than a song lyric. We will experience a peace that quiets all the voices of anxiety, accusation, and anger because God is so present that darkness, pain, sin, and all causes of sorrow are erased. Can that be real? Yes! And when you claim the Savior who provides that eternal reality, you have the sure hope of eternity that lights the paths of the dark valleys of this earth and provides songs of joy that drown the tears and terrors of the worst nightmares.

A dear friend who suffers from Lou Gehrig's disease (ALS) wrote the following to me not long ago:

> Today is bringing us closer to seeing Jesus face-to-face. Depending on Jesus is the only way to live today. He is Life and Light in this dark world. With thirty-five wonderful years of marriage, thirty-four years with ALS, and now thirty years on a ventilator, my purpose for still living is to keep proclaiming the eternal hope I have in Jesus.
>
> Jesus' submission to the greatest suffering of all time has transformed my suffering into momentary light affliction, "producing an eternal weight of glory far beyond all comparison." I am filled with love and joy and peace. There are lots of uncertainties for Susie [his wife] and me, but the nearness of Jesus is bringing incomprehensible comfort and peace which "will guard our hearts and minds in Christ Jesus." It is well with my soul.

You too, dear reader, must always remember not only that the Lord is near but that you are getting nearer and nearer to the full experience of the loving plan of the One who already dwells with you by his Spirit. He will also be with you until that time when there is no more death or pain or fears or tears.

My special-needs brother, who is in prison, recently celebrated a birthday. He's younger than I am, but his body is wearing out. He has heart issues and doesn't have the mental capacity to understand many things. But he does understand the love of Jesus— and by God's wonderful grace, through the severe mercy of being jailed, my brother loves Jesus! Do you know what that means? It means that one day my brother will walk the new earth with more glory than the angels, his mind fully functioning, his body made whole, and his heart made pure.

Pastor Paul Tripp writes, "Thousands of years into eternity, as you're living in a perfect world that has been made new in every way, you'll look back on what now seems unbearable and inescapable as a brief flash of difficulty. There will be a day when you will look back at today, and it will look like a little thing."[3] Knowing that doesn't take away all the pain, but it does give us grace to endure.

The apostle Paul helps us know how the blessings of our future enable us to deal with today's realities. He writes,

> We are afflicted in every way, but not crushed; perplexed, but not driven to despair; persecuted, but not forsaken; struck down, but not destroyed. . . . So we do not lose heart. Though our outer self is wasting away, our inner self is being renewed day by day. For this light momentary affliction is preparing for us an eternal weight of glory beyond all comparison, as we look not to the things that are seen but to the things that are unseen. For the things that are seen are transient, but the things that are unseen are eternal. (2 Cor. 4:8–9, 16–18)

A World Focused on the City of God

Much of Revelation 21 is devoted to describing the new Jerusalem that comes down from heaven:

> Then came one of the seven angels who had the seven bowls full of the seven last plagues and spoke to me. . . . And he carried me away in the Spirit to a great, high mountain, and showed me the holy city Jerusalem coming down out of heaven from God, having the glory of God, its radiance like a most rare jewel, like a jasper, clear as crystal. (vv. 9–11)

In John's vision, the angel shows him a Jerusalem he can recognize. It has a wall with twelve entry gates named for the twelve tribes of Israel, and the foundation stones bear the names of the apostles (John himself, and his friends). But there the familiarity ends. John adds,

> The angel who talked with me had a measuring rod of gold to measure the city, its gates and its walls. The city was laid out like a square, as long as it was wide. He measured the city with the rod and found it to be 12,000 stadia [1,400 miles] in length, and as wide and high as it is long. The angel measured the wall using human measurement, and it was 144 cubits [200 feet] thick. (Rev. 21:15–17 NIV)

This description indicates that the new Jerusalem with its walls is a perfect cube whose measurements echo the perfection of God's will as he welcomes his people to his city. I encourage you not to worry about calculating the specific number of people that can fit in such a space as some have tried to do. Surely the purpose of the perfect numbers is to represent the incalculable perfections of the heavenly Jerusalem that will be our eternal home.

David once sat on the throne in Jerusalem, but a greater King, the divine Seed of David, will sit on the throne in this new Jerusalem. He has already been described in John's vision as the Lion of Judah, a descendant of David, and the Lamb of God (Rev. 5:5–6). He's the King who fulfills the promises to Abraham and his descendants, to David and his offspring, and to all people who need a perfect sacrifice for their sins. John exults in the appearance of this King "who was seated on the throne [and who] said, 'Behold, I am making all things new.'" This King wants John to share his good news with us and commands him, "Write this down, for these words are trustworthy and true" (Rev. 21:5).

What does this King want us to know? What does he ensure John records back in the first century and declares as "trustworthy and true" for all eternity? The One who sits on the throne wants to assure us that he can make all things new in the world and in us. He can give the world and us a clean slate and a fresh start. What an amazing grace! What a divine blessing! The physical glories of the new heaven and earth—the streets of gold, the shining city, the absence of darkness—are a mirror of the spiritual glories of the new us. All our sins and sorrows will be removed. The soul perfections that once only characterized Jesus will then be true of us too. Guilt and shame and even the ability to be tempted will be left behind in the dust of the earth we once knew.

All the things that drive us to betray God, our loved ones, and our own principles for the sake of temporal satisfactions will be gone. In Revelation 21:6, the King declares how the eternal kingdom he will build completes his gracious purpose for us: "It is done! I am the Alpha and the Omega, the beginning and the end. To the thirsty I will give from the spring of the water of life without payment." Throughout our lives we have thirsted for something that money, fame, power, or anything else on earth could not quench. So often we have sacrificed truth, integrity, re-lationships, reputation, and self-respect to find satisfaction apart from God. Yet, despite our repeated quests for significance and self-fulfillment, we discover over and over that whoever tries to find satisfaction in the wells of this world stays empty. Only Jesus himself can satisfy our deepest longings, and in our eternal home he promises to do so.

In the context of this promised provision, the King then says something quite perplexing: "The one who *conquers* will have this heritage, and I will be his God and he will be my son. But as for the cowardly, the faithless, the detestable, as for murderers, the sexu-ally immoral, sorcerers, idolaters, and all liars, their portion will be in the lake that burns with fire and sulfur, which is the second death" (vv. 7–8). Other translations say that those who "overcome" or are "victorious" over all these sins and weaknesses are those who will be included in the blessings of the new heaven and earth.

I think I just got excluded. I think you just got excluded too. If only those who conquer or overcome the sins listed in verse 8 get to enter the city, I guess we all miss the bus. But in reality there is only one person in the Bible who has fully conquered sin. John told us about him earlier in Revelation 5:5: "Weep no more; behold, the Lion of the tribe of Judah, the Root of David, has conquered, so that he can open the scroll and its seven seals [that contain the message of eternity's blessings]." The One who has conquered earth's limitations to secure a sinless, guiltless, painless, and perfectly peaceful eternity is Jesus.

Does that mean that he is the only one in the city? Of course not. In Revelation 12:10–11, John explains:

> And I heard a loud voice in heaven, saying, "Now the salvation and the power and the kingdom of our God and the authority of his Christ have come, for the accuser of our brothers has been thrown down, who accuses them day and night before our God. And *they have conquered* him by the blood of the Lamb and by the word of their testimony, for they loved not their lives even unto death."

Those who have conquered this world's evil and their own temptations so that they can enter the gates of the new Jerusalem are those made able "by the blood of the Lamb." As Jesus's life courses through their veins, they both die for him and live because of him. They conquer death through him.

John makes it even clearer who these conquerors (or overcomers) are in a letter he wrote prior to authoring Revelation: "For everyone who has been born of God overcomes the world. And this is the victory that has overcome the world—our faith. Who is it that overcomes the world except the one who believes that Jesus is the Son of God?" (1 John 5:4–5). Those who have eternity with Jesus are not the ones trusting in their merits but the ones who have faith in his mercy. We don't overcome sin by our perfection but by faith in Christ's provision.

This is the ancient and dear gospel we love and need so much. Those who enter Christ's kingdom are qualified not by their accomplishments but by his. They claim his promises not by commitments to do better but by confidence in his finished work. We triumph over our sins not by our own sweat or tears but by his blood. We overcome guilt and shame not by our efforts, resolutions, or sincere remorse but by resting on the promise of God to make us right with himself by receiving the pardon the Lamb alone makes possible. Believe that Jesus died for your sin on the cross and conquered your guilt by his resurrection, and you'll be saved for all eternity.

A World Filled with God's Glory

The final six verses of Revelation 21 are so rich in integrated meaning that it's best to consider them together.

In verse 22 John says, "I saw no temple in the city, for its temple is the Lord God the Almighty and the Lamb." Why no temple? Because all the sacrificing is done. On the cross Jesus fully atoned for the sins of all who trust in him. He sacrificed himself once for all—One for all. It is finished! God will dwell among his people with nothing between us and him—not sin, grief, distance, expectation, or fear. Sin and sorrow will have vanished. Jesus will be forever present as the eternal Immanuel, "God with us."

"The city has no need of sun or moon to shine on it, for the glory of God gives it light, and its lamp is the Lamb" (v. 23). There will be no darkness in that world or in our souls anymore. The glory of God revealed by the grace of Jesus will have banished darkness forever.

"By its light will the nations walk, and the kings of the earth will bring their glory into it" (v. 24). The light of the Savior isn't only for me or for you or for people of a certain tribe, language, race, or nation. Boundaries and bigotries will be the abandoned flaws of the earth we knew. People from all nations who come to honor their Savior will stream as one holy people into the city of the Lamb for our future eternity. Loved ones and enemies, friends and total strangers, the living and the resurrected dead—all who have been united to Christ by faith will gather for the biggest, best, and longest family reunion ever known, with deeper love uniting us than we have ever experienced.

"Its gates will never be shut by day—and there will be no night there" (v. 25). The gates of the city of our Savior will be open only during daylight hours, but that's not a problem because there will be no night there! The gates will be open for us. No one will be denied entry no matter how dark their sin or circumstances in this life. You will be welcomed to walk through the gates of the new Jerusalem justified by faith in the blood of Jesus regardless of your past background, region, race, or religion.

"The glory and the honor of the nations will be brought into it" (v. 26 NIV). All that's glorious in this world will be brought to honor the Lamb who sits upon the throne. But their glory will pale in comparison to the One sitting on the throne. Mercy and compassion will radiate in the glory and majesty of the One who created the stars and rules for eternity. He will give us endless days of endless praise, as all hours and years will be filled with the joys he provides that will never darken or diminish. We will be able to answer Tolkien's famous question "Is everything sad going to come untrue?" with a joyous "YES!" that will echo through eternity.[4]

Such wonderful blessings are beyond our ability to comprehend fully, but this we know: to miss these blessings is to miss out on the most exquisite provision of love the human heart could ever know. So John ends his vision with a warning: "But nothing unclean will ever enter it, nor anyone who does what is detestable or false, but only those who are written in the Lamb's book of life" (v. 27). This is not to put off or put down anyone but to be honest about the contrast between an eternity with Jesus and one without him. If Jesus didn't love us, he wouldn't have warned us this way.

How can you know if your name is written in the Lamb's book of life? There's only one way to be sure. Trust in Christ's provision for you. Believe that he shed his blood to pay the penalty for your sin and to cleanse you from its guilt. Rejoice that he paid this price for your redemption. Have confidence that he welcomes all who have received him into the new heaven and the new earth. If you trust that Jesus provided what you need for God's acceptance, the gates of the eternal city are wide open for you now and forever!

Digging Deeper

Summaries and Resources for
Understanding Major Millennial Views

Premillennialism

Premillennialism holds that Christ will return after a long period of spiritual decline, which will then be followed by a period of worldwide peace and righteousness lasting for a thousand years. During this time of peace, Christ will reign as King on this earth before returning a final time to conquer evil, carry out the last judgment, and establish his eternal kingdom.

Dispensational Premillennialism (see chart on p. 238) divides the second coming into two parts. First, there is a secret rapture in which the church of living and dead believers are caught up to meet the Lord in the air as he is returning to earth. This first return and resurrection is followed by seven years of tribulation during which the antichrist appears first as an agent of good and then does great

---

For an older but still excellent summary of the major views, see William Arnett, "The Second Coming: Millennial Views," *Christianity Today*, August 31, 1962, https://www.christianitytoday.com/ct/1962/august-31/basic-christian-doctrines -41-second-comingmillennial-views.html.

evil while claiming to be divine. There is also a great conversion of the Jews during this time. Second, Christ returns again to rescue those converted during the tribulation and to reign on earth with all believers, including those he raises from the dead who have died in the tribulation. With these, Christ defeats the antichrist and the forces of evil at the battle of Armageddon, resulting in a thousand years of unprecedented peace and righteousness under Christ's reign. At the close of this millennium, Satan has a little season of final rebellion before the remaining dead are raised in a final resurrection prior to the final judgment, which introduces the eternal state of hell for unbelievers and heaven for believers.

Traditional Dispensationalism holds to (1) the necessity of a separate plan for Israel and the church; (2) a parenthetical age for the church that the Old Testament prophets did not anticipate; and (3) a secret rapture to remove the church from the world prior to a great tribulation in which God will reinstigate his agenda for Israel. Progressive Dispensationalists question or reject the traditional understanding of each of these three distinctions. There are smaller camps within Dispensationalism that teach the rapture will occur after or during the tribulation.

Historic Premillennialism (see chart on p. 239) also holds that the second coming of Christ will come before the millennium. However, this view doesn't contend that God has a separate agenda for Israel and the church, but rather that the church is the intended outcome of God's covenant plan for all nations that began with Israel. As a consequence, Historic Premillennialists don't teach that a secret rapture takes the church out of the world prior to the tribulation so God can execute a separate plan of salvation for Jews. Historic Premillennialists believe all believers go through periods of tribulation, one of which will include the appearance of the antichrist sometime in the future. This tribulation is followed by a rescuing rapture of living and dead believers who then join Christ in his return to earth for a millennial reign of a literal thousand years prior to a final, brief rebellion of Satan that climaxes with the battle of Armageddon, the resurrection of the unbelieving dead, the final judgment, and the assignment of the wicked and the justified to their eternal states.

Amillennialism

An Amillennial view (or perhaps better represented as a Now-Millennium view) teaches that we're in the millennium now (see chart on p. 240). In essence, this view doesn't hold that there will be a literal, thousand-year kingdom of Christ established before or after his second coming. Instead, advocates of Amillennialism think that Christ's spiritual, millennial rule was established by his death and resurrection victory over sin. Now the controlling power of Satan over this world and our hearts has been broken (though many still yield to it). So Christ's kingdom and Satan's kingdom are at war and will continue to be at war until Christ's second coming. Christians and the church are called to prepare for Christ's coming through their increasing influence, witness, and mission that makes his character and care known throughout the earth. At a time known only to God and that most furthers his glory, Jesus will physically return to earth from heaven. This second coming of Christ will be preceded by a significant time of tribulation that includes the evil of an antichrist, whom Christ and his people will defeat in the battle of Armageddon. Then the resurrection of the justified and the wicked will occur, followed by the judgment of the living and dead with all appropriately assigned to their eternal state in heaven or hell based on whether they have faith in Christ.

Postmillennialism

Postmillennialists have the understanding that we're in the end times now (see chart on p. 241) and that the kingdom of Christ began with the death and resurrection events of Jesus's earthly ministry that bound Satan to a limited influence over the world. As a result, the kingdom is being extended in this present era through the preaching of the gospel and the work of the Holy Spirit.

This view holds that, over what may be a lengthy period of time, the world will get better and better under the influence of Christian witness and work, which will ultimately usher in the second coming of Christ. Christ will come when the church's "Christianizing" work on earth is done. This advance of the gospel over time will yield a golden age of peace and righteousness on earth that the Bible identifies as the millennium prior to the second coming. This thousand-year era is more of a symbolic reference to Christ's perfecting influence on the world than a literal number of years.

Advocates of this view expect that the largest proportion of the world's population ultimately will be Christianized during this golden age as the prelude to Christ's return. At the conclusion of the golden age, there will be a brief period of apostasy and rebellion organized by the antichrist. God's people will be rescued from this evil by Jesus's physical return to earth from heaven. Following the defeat of the antichrist, Jesus will empower the resurrection of the justified and the wicked, followed by the judgment of the living and dead with all appropriately assigned to their eternal state in heaven or hell based on whether they have faith in Christ.

Traditional Dispensational Premillennialism

Helpful Image

- Stopwatch

Distinctive Teaching

- Seven dispensations of testing and judgment climaxing in the millennial reign of Christ.
- "Separate and unique" plans for Israel and the church.
- Secret rapture (pre-, mid-, or post-tribulation) prior to second coming.
- Literal thousand-year millennium to convert Jews and unbelieving world.

Key Influences and Development

- Mid-1800s John Nelson Darby
- Scofield Reference Bible (esp. 1917 edition); Ryrie Study Bible (1978)
- *The Late Great Planet Earth* by Hal Lindsey; evangelical dominance from the 1950s to 1990s
- The Left Behind series by Tim LaHaye and Jerry Jenkins

Historic Institutions of Dominant Thought

- Moody Bible Institute, Biola University and Talbot School of Theology, Dallas Theological Seminary, The Master's Seminary, Grace Theological Seminary

Key Proponents

- John Nelson Darby, C. I. Scofield, Charles Ryrie, Lewis Sperry Chafer, A. C. Gaebelein, John Walvoord, J. Dwight Pentecost, J. Vernon McGee, Charles Feinberg, Hal

Lindsey, Tim LaHaye, Jerry Jenkins, David Jeremiah, and John MacArthur (who identifies as a "leaky Dispensationalist," adopting some but not all traditional Dispensational distinctions)

Key Passages

- Predicting a thousand-year millennium and provision for Israel: Gen. 12:1–3; 15:18; Isa. 11; Dan. 9:24–27; Matt. 24:41; Rom. 9–11; 16:25; Rev. 20–21

Interpretive Approach

- *Literal* interpretation, especially regarding Israel (though Ryrie prefers to use the terminology of "plain" or "normal" for fairness and accuracy). Identifies OT prophecies and passages as sparsely symbolic and mostly chronological, applying primarily to ethnic Israel.
- Biblical prophecy provides explicit means to map our time in the last days.

Progressive Dispensational Premillennialism

Helpful Image

- Stopwatch (somewhat less applicable than for traditional Dispensationalists)

Distinctive Teaching

- The kingdom of God is the unifying theme of biblical history.
- One program for both Israel and the church.
- Christ has already inaugurated the Davidic reign in heaven, although he doesn't yet reign as Davidic king on earth.
- Within biblical history there are four dispensational eras, not seven.
- The new covenant has already been inaugurated, though its blessings are not fully realized until the millennium.
- Holistic redemption.

Key Influences and Development

- Dispensational Study Group of the Evangelical Theological Society
- The research and writings of Craig Blaising, Darrell Bock, and Robert Saucy

Institutions of Dominant Thought

- Dallas Theological Seminary, Talbot Seminary, Moody Bible Institute, and Cornerstone Seminary (formerly Grand Rapids Theological Seminary)

Key Proponents

- Darrell Bock, Craig Blaising, Robert Saucy

Key Passages

- Thousand-year millennium on earth prior to Christ's final return with nations engrafted according to God's eternal plan: Gen. 12:2; 22:18; Ruth; Ps. 117; Acts 2:16–21; Rom. 15:4–13

Interpretive Approach

- Literal and complementary hermeneutic.

Historic Premillennialism

Helpful Image

- Atomic Clock

Distinctive Teaching

- Covenant of grace unfolding over time and culminating in Christ.
- Coordinated plans of Israel and the church, with gentiles engrafted; some key advocates contend specific promises remain for ethnic Israel, maintaining literal interpretation.
- "Real" millennium to vindicate Christ's rule and the persecuted church.
- Rapture accompanies the second coming but is not secret.

Key Influences and Development

- Early Church Fathers of the second and third centuries, including Irenaeus, Polycarp, Justin Martyr, and Papias

Key Institutions of Dominant Thought

- Seminaries with some faculty who now hold or have historically held this view: Fuller Theological Seminary, Trinity Evangelical Divinity School, Denver Seminary, Covenant Seminary

Key Proponents

- Dean Alford, Nathaniel West, S. H. Kellogg, George Eldon Ladd, Walter Martin, John Warwick Montgomery, R. Laird Harris, J. Barton Payne, Wilbur Wallis, Craig Blomberg

Key Passages

- Thousand-year millennium follows prophesied engrafting of the gentiles: Gen. 12:2; 22:18; Isa. 7:14; 11; Luke 2:29–32; Acts 2:16–21; Rom. 9–11; 15:4–13; 1 Thess. 4; 2 Thess. 2:3; Rev. 20–21

Interpretive Approach

- Natural interpretation—that is, as literal as context makes appropriate to indicate whether symbolism is intended (e.g., "Great beast," "Lamb," "Babylon"); mostly chronological.

Amillennialism

Helpful Image

- Cornucopia of Grace

Distinctive Teaching

- Thousand-year reign symbolic of a Covenantal view unfolding in church age.
- Satan bound in Christ's death, resurrection, and ascension.
- Promises to Israel are fulfilled in the church.
- Final apostasy (includes Armageddon preceding second coming).

Key Influences and Development

- Augustine (but he was also Postmillennial in some respects)
- Majority of Christians in majority of Christian Era

Institutions of Dominant Thought

- Majority of world's Christian institutions (including Roman Catholic, Lutheran, Reformed, and some Baptists)
- Reformed Theological Seminary, Westminster Theological Seminary, Covenant Theological Seminary, Calvin Theological Seminary, Knox Theological Seminary, Puritan Reformed Seminary, Mid-America Reformed Seminary, Gordon-Conwell Theological Seminary

Key Proponents

- Augustine, Louis Berkhof, Geerhardus Vos, John Murray, Abraham Kuyper, William Hendriksen, J. I. Packer,

Michael Horton, Anthony Hoekema, R. C. Sproul (originally), Tim Keller, Sam Storms

Key Passages

- Blessings to the nations *fulfill* promises to Israel: Isa. 2:2–4; Matt. 24:21; Acts 2:30–32; Rom. 9:6–7; Gal. 3:29; 2 Thess. 2:6–8; Rev. 6; 12; 20:4

Interpretive Approach

- Direct or natural interpretation (literal and symbolic) determined by literary intent.
- Progressive parallelism in Revelation.
- Prophecy is intended to be comfort and inspiration for persecuted churches and instruction for the mission of the church.

Postmillennialism

Helpful Image

- Hill Climb

Distinctive Teaching

- Covenant theology unfolding over time ("the Long View").
- United plan for Israel and the church (critics say "substitution" or "replacement"; advocates say "engrafting").
- "Golden age" millennium ushers in Christ's return.

Key Influences and Development

- Any era of Christian dominance (e.g., the Crusades, England at the time of "British Israelism," colonial and nineteenth-century America)
- Many Anglo/American evangelicals before Dispensationalism (reflecting "Manifest Destiny" mindset)
- Many Anglo/American evangelicals before World War I

Institutions of Dominant Thought (among Evangelicals)

- Puritan roots and "Old" Princeton
- Theonomic schools teaching Theocratic Reform, Federal Vision, Christian Nationalism, etc.
- Charismatic/Pentecostal schools teaching Latter Rain theology, dominion theology, etc.

Key Proponents

- Augustine (but he was also Amillennial in some respects), Charles Hodge, A. A. Hodge, B. B. Warfield, W. G. T. Shedd, Robert Dabney, Augustus Strong, Benjamin

Warfield, Loraine Boettner, Iain Murray, D. James Kennedy, J. Jefferson Davis

- Theonomy: R. J. Rushdoony, Greg Bahnsen, Gary North, Ken Gentry, Doug Wilson
- Charismatic/Pentecostal: Paul Yongli Cho, Kenneth Copeland, John Hagee, Pat Robertson

Key Passages

- Christ's rule was prophesied to all and will extend over all: Pss. 22; 67; 110; Isa. 2:2–4; 11:9; Hab. 2:14; Matt. 13:31–33; Luke 20:9–16; John 12:31–32; Rom. 9:6; 11:25–27; Gal. 3; 6:16–17; Eph. 2:12–18

Interpretive Approach

- Revelation and other prophetic passages are literal and spiritual with descriptive vignettes (not necessarily chronological but often symbolic) of final events and the eternal kingdom.
- Prophecy is intended to be instruction and comfort for the persecuted church.

Questions for Review and Discussion

Introduction

1. Do you believe that Jesus is coming back?
2. What do you expect will happen *when* he comes?
3. What do you think will happen *before* he comes?
4. How do you feel about people who have different views from yours regarding what will happen before Jesus returns?
5. What do you think your attitude should be toward those who believe that Jesus died for their sins, rose in victory over sin, and is coming again in power and great glory— but have different opinions about what will happen before he comes again?
6. How do you expect this book will talk about Christians who have different views of what will happen *before* Jesus returns but are confident that he *will* return?
7. How can we differ on views of the last days and still unite in Christ's mission?
8. What are basic questions that you have about the last days prior to Christ's return?

Chapter 1: Are We Living in the Last Days?

1. What do most people mean when they talk about the last days?
2. What are some popular impressions that you know people have about what will happen in the last days? Where do people get these impressions?
3. What happens to our credibility or others' faith when people try to predict exactly when Jesus will return?
4. How does the language and content of Revelation make precise predictions of Jesus's return difficult? Why do you think the Holy Spirit inspired this difficulty in God's Word?
5. How often do you think people have predicted that we are in the last days before Jesus comes back? Are such predictions always wrong?
6. How does the Bible describe the last days?
7. What are some key Bible passages that tell us when the last days are?
8. When do (or did) the last days begin?
9. What are some things that will happen in the last days before Jesus returns?
10. Is Jesus coming back "soon"?

Chapter 2: Expectations for the End Times

1. What are some things that the Bible tells us will occur in the last days?
2. Are the wars that Jesus predicted prior to his return near or far—or both?
3. What do you think the antichrist will be like? Where did you get your ideas?
4. Is there only one antichrist, or could there be more?

5. Who have been some candidates for the antichrist in the past?

6. Do you think that the main antichrist predicted in Scripture has already come in the past, is already living on earth, or is yet to come?

7. How does the rebirth of the nation of Israel affect your thinking about when Jesus will return?

8. Have there been other rebirths of Israel in the past? If so, how do those rebirths affect your thinking about when Jesus will return?

9. Has enough of what the Bible predicts will happen prior to Jesus's return already occurred to make you think Jesus could return soon?

Chapter 3: Views of Previous Times

1. What key things do you think must occur before Jesus returns?

2. Could many of these things occur in your lifetime? How is that possible?

3. Could most or all of these things happen very soon? How is that possible?

4. Why is it important not to shrug off any concern that Jesus could come back very soon? If we don't know for sure, does it still matter? Why?

5. How do past views of biblical history affect how one interprets biblical prophecy for the future?

6. Do you lean toward a view that the law in the Old Testament is not as important for us as the gospel of the New Testament? Why?

7. Do you lean toward a view that God had a different plan of salvation for the people in the Old Testament than he does for those of us in the New Testament age? Why?

8. Do you lean toward a view that God has always saved his people by grace that is progressively revealed in the Old Testament and fully revealed in Jesus? Why?

9. How does your view of how the Old Testament relates to the New Testament affect your view of what will happen before Jesus returns?

10. What is the millennium?

11. What are four views of the millennium, and how are they affected by your view of how the Old and New Testaments relate to each other?

Chapter 4: Dispensational Premillennial View

1. What is Dispensationalism? What makes it a Premillennial view?

2. What key principle of Bible interpretation do Dispensationalists insist upon?

3. To what group of people do Dispensationalists believe Old Testament promises and prophecies apply?

4. What are some key prophecies in the book of Daniel that Dispensationalists rejoice to see fulfilled in the New Testament?

5. What is the "great parenthesis" in Old Testament prophecy according to Dispensational thinking?

6. As a consequence of the great parenthesis, what group of people did the Old Testament prophets not foresee being included in God's eternal kingdom?

7. What is the rapture?

8. Why is the *secret* rapture needed in Dispensational thinking? What groups of people are being separated so that God can continue his original salvation plan?

9. What is the tribulation, and why is it important for Jewish people?

10. When did Dispensationalism start being taught in earnest, and what factors caused the reference Bible teaching it to become so popular?

11. What has made Dispensationalism such a popular view in our time?

Chapter 5: Dispensationalism Today

1. Why was Hal Lindsey's *The Late Great Planet Earth* so important in American evangelical culture?

2. What events in the latter half of the twentieth century seemed to fit very well with the ideas in Hal Lindsey's understanding of the last days?

3. What happened near the end of the twentieth century that made Dispensationalists reexamine Scripture to further ground their views in Scripture?

4. How do Progressive Dispensational views differ from those of classical/traditional Dispensationalists on matters such as literal interpretation, the rapture, and the unforeseen church age?

5. What led to these differences? How important is a commitment to Scripture to both Progressive and classical Dispensationalists?

6. How do Progressive Dispensational views align with those of classical Dispensationalism, especially regarding a separate plan of God for Israel?

7. Do Progressive or classical Dispensational views dominate Bible school and preaching today? Why?

8. Do Progressive or classical Dispensational views dominate popular Christian culture? Why?

Chapter 6: Historic Premillennial View, Part 1: People and Perspectives

1. Prior to reading this book, had you ever heard of the Historic Premillennial view?

2. Which people taught the Historic Premillennial view in the age of the early church, and which people have taught it in modern times?

3. What does Historic Premillennialism teach about the timing of Christ's return and the establishment of his eternal kingdom?

4. Do Historic Premillennialists believe that the Old Testament prophets foresaw God extending the gospel to gentiles? Why?

5. Do Historic Premillennialists believe the Bible should be interpreted literally? What does "literal" interpretation mean for Historic Premillennialists?

6. How does their understanding of the unity of the Old and New Testaments affect the way Historic Premillennialists interpret Old Testament prophecies?

7. If there is a unity of the Old and New Testament salvation plan, does the prophetic clock ever need to stop running in order for the church to start and grow?

8. Do you think that God has a different salvation plan for those in Israel and those in the church? If so, what are the differences between those plans?

9. If God has a unified salvation plan for those in Israel and those in the church, then how are all saved? Will they be together or separate in heaven?

Chapter 7: Historic Premillennial View, Part 2: Events

1. What do Historic Premillennialists believe about the rapture?
2. How is the Historic Premillennial understanding of the rapture different from the Dispensational understanding?
3. Do Historic Premillennialists believe in the tribulation? If so, in what sense?
4. How do Historic Premillennialists and Dispensationalists come together in their views of the timing of the millennium?
5. Do Historic Premillennialists believe in a thousand-year reign of Christ and his followers upon the earth? Why?
6. What will be the nature of the millennium according to Historic Premillennialists?
7. Why is it important for Historic Premillennialists that there be a millennium in which believers will reign with Christ upon the earth?
8. What will be the nature of the new heaven and earth according to Historic Premillennialists? Who will be there?
9. With what you now know about Historic Premillennialism and Progressive Dispensationalism, how far apart do you consider these views? Why?

Chapter 8: Amillennial View

1. Is it fair to say that Amillennialists believe that there is no millennium? Why?
2. How can Amillennialists believe that the spiritual realities of the millennium are already present *now*?
3. Which church groups have tended to adopt an Amillennial position?

4. Do Amillennialists believe in a literal interpretation of Scripture? What do they mean by this term?

5. What role do shadow and fulfillment play in the Bible interpretation of Amillennialists?

6. Do Amillennialists tend to view the Old and New Testaments as more of a unified plan of salvation or as separate plans?

7. How do unfolding scriptural covenants affect how Amillennialists interpret biblical prophecy?

8. Do Amillennialists believe in the rapture? In what way?

9. Do Amillennialists believe in the tribulation? In what way?

10. How do Amillennialists interpret and group chapters of the book of Revelation?

11. Do Amillennialists believe that Jesus is coming back? What will happen before he does? What should we do before he returns?

Chapter 9: Postmillennial View

1. When do Postmillennialists tend to think that Christ will return—in a time near or far?

2. When do Postmillennialists think that Jesus will return relative to the millennium—before, during, or after?

3. When do Postmillennialists think the millennium begins?

4. What do Postmillennialists expect will happen in the millennium?

5. How does this expectation affect their view of whether the world will get better or worse prior to Christ's return?

6. How effective do Postmillennialists expect the spread of the gospel to be prior to Christ's return?

7. How are the thousand years of the millennium explained by a golden age according to Postmillennialists? Is the thousand years literal?

8. How does the golden age in Postmillennial thought affect their views of politics and government?

9. What Scripture texts do Postmillennialists use to support their ideas about the spread of the gospel and the growing reign of Christ upon the earth prior to his return?

10. What method of Bible interpretation do Postmillennialists use to explain the millennium described in Revelation 20?

11. Why do some think it is more helpful to be a glass-half-full rather than a glass-half-empty interpreter of the last days that we are in?

Chapter 10: Which View Should I Believe?

1. Should we interpret the prophecies in the Bible literally or spiritually or both?

2. Do any of the major views of prophetic interpretation fail to take into account the context, audience, or content of the Bible when deciding whether an interpretation should be literal or spiritual? Are the "literal" versus "spiritual" labels fair for most Bible-believing interpreters?

3. What interpretive principles should we all use when determining the meaning and fulfillment of biblical prophecy?

4. How does Daniel 9 help us to see the importance of considering the literal and spiritual implications of difficult texts and interpreting them with humility?

5. How do Revelation 19 and 20 help us to see the importance of considering the literal and spiritual implications of difficult texts and interpreting them with humility?

6. How should it affect our reading of Scripture to know that all views require some degree of both literal and spiritual interpretation?

7. How should it affect us to realize that some common views of the last days may require people to believe in

    multiple raptures, resurrections, returns, and heavenly destinies with little in Scripture to indicate more than one of each?

8. How should it affect us to realize that holding to some historic views of the last days may require us to consider Scripture passages out of the order in which they naturally occur in the book of Revelation?

9. How should it affect us to realize that all views in this book believe that God has a plan for Israel, either as a separate people or as members of the body of Christ?

10. Since no one knows with certainty all the details of the last days, how should we relate to fellow Christians who have differing views from our own about the end times?

Chapter 11: The Hope All Christians Share, Part 1: Essentials for Eternity

1. What view of the truth and authority of Scripture does God call all believers to share?

2. Why did Jesus die on the cross?

3. How should we relate to others who believe Jesus died for their sins but hold different ideas about the end times?

4. What do all genuine Christians believe about Jesus's resurrection?

5. What should we believe about others who trust that God raised Jesus from the dead? How should we treat and talk about these fellow believers?

6. How does the Holy Spirit operate in the lives of all believers?

7. How should we treat and talk about those in whom the Holy Spirit dwells?

8. What confidence should we have in fulfilling God's plans for us and in maintaining the heart that he requires of us since we are indwelt by the Holy Spirit?

Chapter 12: The Hope All Christians Share, Part 2: Essentials for the End Times

1. What do all the major millennial views teach about the suffering and persecution of believers in the last days?
2. How should this common understanding of suffering and persecution prepare God's people for Christ's coming?
3. What do all the major millennial views share in their understanding of the rapture that precedes Christ's coming? How should that common ground prepare us for Christ's coming?
4. What do all the major millennial views share in their understanding of the resurrection that accompanies Christ's second coming? How should that common ground prepare us for Christ's coming?
5. What do all of the major millennial views share in their understanding of the final judgment and the punishment of the wicked? How should that common ground prepare us for Christ's coming?
6. What do all of the major millennial views share in their understanding of the new heaven and earth that are ushered in by the last days? How should that common ground prepare us for Christ's coming?
7. How should the hope that all believers share affect our expectations for Christ's coming and our love for one another until he does?

Chapter 13: "Behold, I Am Making All Things New"

1. What will happen to our world after the last days of this earth?

2. What will fill the new heaven and earth after this world is past?

3. What effect will this filling have on the new heaven and earth?

4. What will happen to us after the last days of this earth?

5. What will our existence be like after the last days of this earth?

6. What will our bodies be like after the last days of this earth?

7. What will happen to pain, suffering, and sin after the last days of this earth?

8. What will our loved ones who love Jesus be like after the last days of this earth, and what will our relationship with them be like?

9. What will happen to all of Christ's enemies and evil after the last days of this earth?

10. Who will be in Christ's kingdom after the last days of this earth?

11. What glory will fill Christ's kingdom after the last days of this earth, and what will that be like?

12. How can you know that you will enjoy the peace, pardon, and glory of Christ's eternal kingdom after your last days on this earth?

Charts of Millennial Views

Dispensational Premillennial View of the End Times

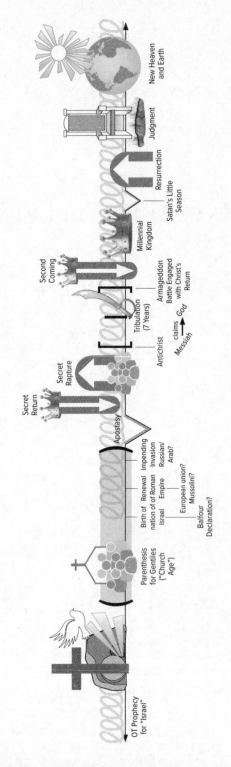

Parenthetical "church age" interrupts the fulfillment of prophetic prediction prior to continued unfolding of God's kingdom purposes.

Historic Premillennial View of the End Times

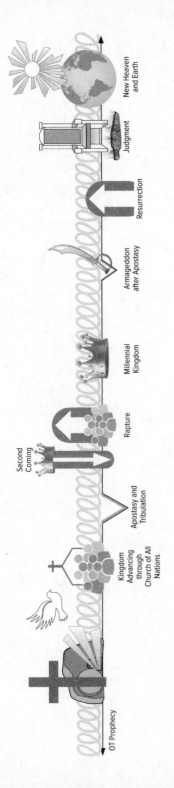

OT Prophecy

Kingdom Advancing through Church of All Nations

Apostasy and Tribulation

Second Coming

Rapture

Millennial Kingdom

Armageddon after Apostasy

Resurrection

Judgment

New Heaven and Earth

Continuous fulfillment of prophetic prediction and Christ's kingdom purposes.

Amillennial View of the End Times

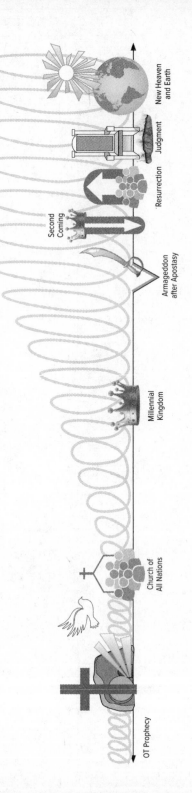

OT Prophecy

Church of All Nations

Millennial Kingdom

Armageddon after Apostasy

Second Coming

Resurrection

Judgment

New Heaven and Earth

Increasing fulfillment of prophetic prediction and Christ's kingdom purposes.

Postmillennial View of the End Times

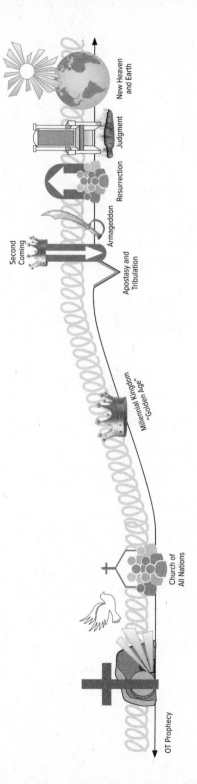

OT Prophecy

Church of All Nations

Millennial Kingdom "Golden Age"

Second Coming

Apostasy and Tribulation

Armageddon

Resurrection

Judgment

New Heaven and Earth

Increasing influence of Christ's kingdom to fulfill prophetic prediction and God's purposes.

Acknowledgments

I am thankful for the leadership of the historic Grace Presbyterian Church in Peoria, Illinois, where I have had the privilege of serving the Lord, proclaiming his Word, being loved by his people, and initially preparing this material for our local congregation and the wider church.

I give thanks for the ministry of Bible Study Fellowship—especially its former executive director Susie Rowan—whose invitation allowed me to organize and present this material to its international and interdenominational leaders. The courage and faith of this Bible-centered organization is a model of what it means to let the Word speak to God's people with fair representation of differing views and firm commitment to the ultimate truth of Scripture.

The skills, generous spirit, and expansive knowledge of writer Jack Kuhatschek were essential for drawing together my notes and lectures into book format so that I could complete the writing of this material.

Karen Frey remains my ever-faithful, hardworking, and sharp-eyed executive assistant. Her organizational skills and godly spirit make the many dimensions of my ministry possible and a daily joy.

Notes

Chapter 1 Are We Living in the Last Days?

1. Dave Barry, "Doomsayer Goofs—But Hey, It's Not the End of the World," *Chicago Tribune*, August 27, 1989, https://www.chicagotribune.com/news/ct-xpm-1989-08-27-8901070982-story.html.

2. Quoted in Anthony A. Hoekema, *The Four Major Cults* (Grand Rapids: Eerdmans, 1963), 90.

3. Hoekema, *Four Major Cults*, 90.

4. Quoted in Hoekema, *Four Major Cults*, 91.

5. Ashley May and Sean Rossman, "World Ending Saturday? Here Are 8 Times the World Was Supposed to End, and Didn't," *USA Today*, September 21, 2017, https://www.usatoday.com/story/news/nation-now/2017/09/21/world-ending-saturday-here-all-times-world-supposed-end-and-didnt/689011001/.

6. Tremper Longman III, ed., *The Baker Illustrated Bible Dictionary*, s.v. "Apocalyptic" (Grand Rapids: Baker Books, 2013), 81–82.

7. George Eldon Ladd, *A Commentary on the Revelation of John* (Grand Rapids: Eerdmans, 1972), 10–12.

8. Gregory Beale, "Why Is the Number of the Beast 666?," Westminster Theological Seminary website, February 11, 2015, https://faculty.wts.edu/posts/why-is-the-number-of-the-beast-666/.

9. Richard J. Krejcir, "The Four Main Views of Revelation," ChurchLeadership.org, http://www.churchleadership.org/apps/articles/default.asp?articleid=43118.

10. Patrick Zukeran, "Four Views of Revelation," Evidence and Answers, November 4, 2012, https://evidenceandanswers.org/article/four-views-revelation/.

11. Zukeran, "Four Views."

12. J. Scott Duvall, *Revelation*, Teach the Text Commentary Series (Grand Rapids: Baker Books, 2014), 6.

13. David Jeremiah, *Is This the End?* (Nashville: W Publishing Group, 2016), back cover.

14. Eckhard Schnabel, *40 Questions about the End Times* (Grand Rapids: Kregel, 2011), 20.

15. Justin Taylor, "Yes, We Really Are Living in the Last Days," The Gospel Coalition, March 31, 2020, https://www.thegospelcoalition.org/blogs/justin-taylor/yes-we-really-are-living-in-the-last-days/.

16. Schnabel, *40 Questions*, 23.

17. Ladd, *Commentary on the Revelation of John*, 13.

18. J. Barton Payne, *Biblical Prophecy for Today* (Grand Rapids: Baker, 1978), 29, 77.

19. Some have recently argued that we cannot simultaneously work for a revival of Christian faithfulness and teach that the world could end at any moment, but most Christians have taken the doctrine of Christ's imminent appearing as a spur to preparedness as well as encouragement to present faithfulness. See Jack Jenkins, "As Christian Nationalism Digs In, Differing Visions Surface," Religious News Service, October 28, 2022, https://religionnews.com/2022/10/28/as-christian-nationalism-digs-in-will-differing-visions-clash/.

20. For an excellent discussion and an inspiring call to faithfulness that Christ's imminent return should stimulate, see John Piper, *Come Lord Jesus: Meditations on the Second Coming of Christ* (Wheaton: Crossway, 2023), 258–59.

Chapter 2 Expectations for the End Times

1. Max J. Lee, "Revelation," in *The Baker Illustrated Bible Commentary*, ed. Gary M. Burge and Andrew Hill (Grand Rapids: Baker Books, 2012), 1614.

2. Dana Netherton, "Historic Premillennialism: Taking the Long View," *Christian History*, issue 61 (1999), https://www.christianitytoday.com/history/issues/issue-61/historic-premillennialism-taking-long-view.html.

3. "A History of the Second Coming: Did You Know?—Hall of Infamy," *Christian History*, issue 61 (1999), https://www.christianitytoday.com/history/issues/issue-61/history-of-second-coming-did-you-know--hall-of-infamy.html.

4. Quoted in Dennis Pettibone, "Martin Luther's Views on the Antichrist," *Journal of the Adventist Theological Society* 18, no. 1 (Spring 2007): 91.

5. "Of the Antichrist," in *Brief Statement of the Doctrinal Position of the Missouri Synod*, adopted 1932 (St. Louis: Concordia, n.d.), 12, https://www.lcms.org/about/beliefs/doctrine/brief-statement-of-lcms-doctrinal-position#anti-christ. For more current discussion within Missouri Synod ranks, see Sean Smith, "Is the Pope the Antichrist?," *Concord Matters* (podcast), November 5, 2019, https://www.kfuo.org/2019/11/05/concord-matters-110519-is-the-pope-the-antichrist/. A similar statement from the Evangelical Lutheran Synod can be found at https://els.org/resources/answers/the-antichrist/.

6. Chris Staron, "Dispensationalism and John Nelson Darby," *Truce* (podcast), season 5, episode 3, March 1, 2022, https://trucepodcast.com/?s=Darby.

7. Ashley Williams, "From Absolute Monarchy to Absolute Demon: 'Identity of Napoleon and Antichrist,'" The Beehive, updated March 14, 2018, https://www.masshist.org/beehiveblog/2018/03/from-absolute-monarchy-to-absolute-demon-identity-of-napoleon-and-antichrist/.

8. Quoted in "History of the Second Coming."

9. Mark Galli, "A History of the Second Coming: From the Editor—Sliver in a Forest," *Christian History*, issue 61 (1999), https://www.christianitytoday.com/history/issues/issue-61/history-of-second-coming-from-editor--sliver-in-forest.html.

10. Netherton, "Historic Premillennialism."

11. Reginald Stackhouse, "Columbus's Millennial Voyage," *Christian History*, issue 61 (1999), https://www.christianitytoday.com/history/issues/issue-61/columbuss-millennial-voyage.html.

12. Quoted in Art Levine, "The Devil in Gorbachev," *Washington Post*, June 5, 1988, https://www.washingtonpost.com/archive/opinions/1988/06/05/the-devil-in-gorbachev/34f9db9b-9498-4894-9800-90f7d3d4e434/.

13. Levine, "The Devil in Gorbachev."

14. Geraldine Fagan, "How the Russian Orthodox Church Is Helping Drive Putin's War in Ukraine," *Time*, April 15, 2022, https://time.com/6167332/putin-russian-orthodox-church-war-ukraine/.

15. History.com Editors, "Jerusalem Captured in First Crusade," History, accessed March 14, 2023, https://www.history.com/this-day-in-history/jerusalem-captured-in-first-crusade.

16. History.com Editors, "Balfour Declaration Letter Written," History, accessed March 14, 2023, https://www.history.com/this-day-in-history/the-balfour-declaration.

17. Yolande Knell, "Balfour Declaration: The Divisive Legacy of 67 Words," BBC News, November 2, 2017, https://www.bbc.com/news/world-middle-east-41765892.

18. "The Arab-Israeli War of 1948," US Department of State Office of the Historian, accessed March 14, 2023, https://history.state.gov/milestones/1945-1952/arab-israeli-war.

19. Chris Mitchell, "Almost Armageddon: Why the Six-Day War Was a Prophetic Milestone," CBN News, May 9, 2017, https://www1.cbn.com/cbnnews/israel/2017/may/why-the-six-day-war-was-a-prophetic-milestone-and-nearly-armageddon.

Chapter 3 Views of Previous Times

1. Winfried Vogel, "The Eschatological Theology of Martin Luther," *Andrews University Seminary Studies* 24, no. 3 (Autumn 1986): 249–64 (esp. 258–60), https://digitalcommons.andrews.edu/cgi/viewcontent.cgi?article=1791&context=auss.

2. Charles C. Ryrie, *Dispensationalism Today* (Chicago: Moody, 1965), 132.

Chapter 4 Dispensational Premillennial View

1. Quoted from promo copy for the book *Left Behind* by Tim LaHaye and Jerry B. Jenkins (Carol Stream, IL: Tyndale, 1995).

2. Thanks to Scott Spuler, owner, developer, and designer at OneHat Technologies, LLC, for the concept art and development of the charts in this book. I am very appreciative of his faith, expertise, and skills that are on rich display here. It is important for readers to note that the charts are designed to present sequences of events rather than to proportionally represent periods of time.

3. Quoted in Charles C. Ryrie, "What Is a Dispensation?," accessed March 23, 2023, http://www.gracebiblestudies.org/Resources/Web/www.duluthbible.org/g_f_j/Dispensationalism_1.htm.

4. Quoted in Charles C. Ryrie, *Dispensationalism*, rev. ed. (Chicago: Moody, 1995), 39.

5. Ryrie, *Dispensationalism*, 80–81.

6. Ryrie, *Dispensationalism*, 82.

7. Floyd E. Hamilton, *The Basis of Millennial Faith* (Grand Rapids: Eerdmans, 1942), 38.

8. See Precept Austin, "Daniel 9:25 Commentary," last updated December 31, 2022, https://www.preceptaustin.org/daniel_925#9:25, where a variety of experts offer this date. However, any internet search will quickly reveal a number of alternative dates for the decree of Artaxerxes.

9. Arnold Fruchtenbaum, "The Messianic Time Table According to Daniel the Prophet," Jews for Jesus, April 20, 2018, https://jewsforjesus.org/learn/the-messianic-time-table-according-to-daniel-the-prophet/.

10. For a wonderfully researched supporting view that precisely ties Daniel's prediction to crucifixion and resurrection events, see Rodger C. Young, "The Theological Problem Presented by the Exactness of Daniel's 70 Weeks," *Journal of the Evangelical Theological Society* 65, no. 3 (September 2022): 473–89. Immediately following in this same journal is a well-argued article presenting a case for Daniel's 70 weeks being better understood when representing an approximate fulfillment. See David Larson, "Approximate Fulfillment as the Key to Reconsidering the Decree of Cyrus as the Beginning Point of Daniel's 70 Weeks," *Journal of the Evangelical Theological Society* 65, no. 3 (September 2022): 491–507.

11. Tim LaHaye, *The Rapture: Who Will Face the Tribulation?* (Eugene, OR: Harvest House, 2002), 39.

12. Jeremiah, *Is This The End?*, 241. Some Dispensationalists believe that the rapture will occur in the middle of the tribulation, while others believe it will occur at the end of the tribulation. However, the pretribulation view has always been the dominant view.

Chapter 5 Dispensationalism Today

1. Hal Lindsey, *The Late Great Planet Earth* (Grand Rapids: Zondervan, 1970), 53–54.

2. Joshua J. Mark, "Kingdom of Israel," World History Encyclopedia, October 26, 2018, https://www.worldhistory.org/Kingdom_of_Israel/.

3. Lindsey, *Late Great Planet Earth*, 52–53.

4. Hal Lindsey, *The 1980s: Countdown to Armageddon* (King of Prussia, PA: Westgate Press, 1980), 8.

5. Jeremiah, *Is This The End?*, 171.

6. Jeremiah, *Is This The End?*, 172.

7. John F. Walvoord, *End Times Prophecy: Ancient Wisdom for Uncertain Times* (Colorado Springs: David C Cook, 2016), 42.

8. Britt Gillette, *The End Times: A Guide to Bible Prophecy and the Last Days* (self-pub., 2019), chap. 3, p. 3, Google Books.

9. John Walvoord, "The Second Coming of Christ and the Millennial Kingdom," Bible.org, accessed March 14, 2023, https://bible.org/seriespage/15-second-coming-christ-and-millennial-kingdom.

10. Ron Rhodes, *The End Times in Chronological Order: A Complete Overview to Understanding Bible Prophecy* (Eugene, OR: Harvest House, 2012), 188.

11. John F. Walvoord, *End Times Prophecy*, 95.

12. Some Dispensationalists believe the church will be in heaven during the millennium.

13. "Where Will We Spend Eternity? Heaven or Earth?," Grace Bible Church (Warren, MI), August 25, 2019, https://rightlydividing.org/articles/eternity/where-will-we-spend-eternity-heaven-or-earth/. Emphasis added.

14. Craig Blaising, Ken Gentry Jr., and Robert Strimple, *Three Views on the Millennium and Beyond*, ed. Darrell L. Bock, Counterpoints Bible and Theology (Grand Rapids: Zondervan, 1999), 185–86.

15. John MacArthur, *The Glory of Heaven* (Wheaton: Crossway, 1996), 89.

16. Craig A. Blaising and Darrell L. Bock, *Dispensationalism, Israel and the Church: The Search for Definition* (Grand Rapids: Zondervan, 1992); Craig A. Blaising and Darrell L. Bock, *Progressive Dispensationalism* (Wheaton: BridgePoint, 1993); Robert L. Saucy, *The Case for Progressive Dispensationalism* (Grand Rapids: Zondervan, 1993).

17. Ryrie, *Dispensationalism*, 164–65.

18. Blaising and Bock, *Progressive Dispensationalism*, 52.

19. Blaising and Bock, *Dispensationalism, Israel and the Church*, 392–93, 59.

20. Blaising and Bock, *Progressive Dispensationalism*, 47.

21. Ryrie, *Dispensationalism*, 39.

22. See Ryrie's statement of God's different plan for Israel and the Church as a *sine qua non* (i.e., a truth essential for the system to exist) of Dispensationalism in the first editions of *Dispensationalism Today*, 44.

23. Ryrie, *Dispensationalism*, 167.

24. Wikipedia, s.v. "Progressive Dispensationalism," last edited September 28, 2022, https://en.wikipedia.org/wiki/Progressive_dispensationalism.

25. Blaising and Bock, *Progressive Dispensationalism*, 208.

26. Blaising and Bock, *Progressive Dispensationalism*, 56.

27. Robert L. Thomas, "The Hermeneutics of Progressive Dispensationalism," *The Master's Seminary Journal* 6, no. 1 (Spring 1995): 79–80.

28. "Interview with a Premillennialist, Dr. Darrell Bock," *The Christian Post*, July 18, 2005, https://www.christianpost.com/news/interview-with-a-premillennialist-dr -darrell-bock.html.

Chapter 6 Historic Premillennial View, Part 1

1. Netherton, "Historic Premillennialism."

2. Robert G. Clouse, "Introduction," in *The Meaning of the Millennium: Four Views*, ed. Robert G. Clouse (Downers Grove, IL: IVP Academic, 1977), 9.

3. A. Skevington Wood, "The Eschatology of Irenaeus," *Evangelical Quarterly* (1969), 41.

4. George Eldon Ladd, "Historic Premillennialism," in *Meaning of the Millennium*, 17–18.

5. Ladd, "Historic Premillennialism," 27. See also J. Barton Payne, *Encyclopedia of Biblical Prophecy* (New York: Harper and Row, 1973), 106–7.

6. Ladd, "Historic Premillennialism," 23.

7. Ladd, "Historic Premillennialism," 20–21, italics in original.

8. Payne, *Encyclopedia of Biblical Prophecy*, 128–29.

9. Payne, *Encyclopedia of Biblical Prophecy*, 20, 24.

10. Payne, *Biblical Prophecy for Today*, 54–55.

Chapter 7 Historic Premillennial View, Part 2

1. Payne, *Biblical Prophecy for Today*, 50–51.

2. Schnabel, *40 Questions*, 94.

3. Payne, *Biblical Prophecy for Today*, 44–46.

4. Ladd, "Historic Premillennialism," 17.

5. Michael W. Holmes, *1 & 2 Thessalonians*, NIV Application Commentary (Grand Rapids: Zondervan, 1998), 151.

6. Payne, *Biblical Prophecy for Today*, 17–18.

7. Payne, *Biblical Prophecy for Today*, 19.

8. Payne, *Biblical Prophecy for Today*, 60–63.

9. Craig L. Blomberg, "The Posttribulationism of the New Testament: Leaving 'Left Behind' Behind," in *A Case for Historic Premillennialism*, ed. Craig L. Blomberg and Sung Wook Chung (Grand Rapids: Baker Academic, 2009), 123, Kindle.

10. Ladd, *Commentary on the Revelation of John*, 14.

11. Payne, *Biblical Prophecy for Today*, 21–22.

12. Ladd, "Historic Premillennialism," 33.

13. Payne, *Biblical Prophecy for Today*, 24–25.

14. Blomberg, "Posttribulationism of the New Testament," 116.

15. Ladd, "Historic Premillennialism," 17.

16. Schnabel, *40 Questions*, 268–69.

17. Payne, *Encyclopedia of Biblical Prophecy*, 115–16.

18. Wilbur B. Wallis, *The Coming of the Kingdom: A Survey of the Book of Revelation*, reprinted from the Covenant Seminary journal *Presbyterion* (Spring, 1982; rev. 1992), 69.

19. Ladd, *Commentary on the Revelation of John*, 268, 272. See also Cornelius P. Venema, "What about Revelation 20, Part 1," *Reformed Perspectives Magazine* 9, no. 50 (December 9–15, 2007), https://thirdmill.org/newfiles/cor_venema/cor_venema .Revelation20.a.html.

Chapter 8 Amillennial View

1. David Jeremiah, "What Is the Millennium? 7 Answers to 7 Questions," David Jeremiah.blog, accessed March 16, 2023, https://davidjeremiah.blog/what-is-the-millen nium-7-answers-to-7-questions/.

2. John Walvoord, *The Millennial Kingdom: A Basic Text in Premillennial Theology* (Grand Rapids: Zondervan Academic, 1983), 61.

3. Robert B. Strimple, "Amillennialism," in *Three Views*, 83.

4. Strimple, "Amillennialism," 86.

5. Strimple, "Amillennialism," 89.

6. "Replacement Theology," Gateway Center for Israel, accessed March 16, 2023, https://centerforisrael.com/papers/replacement-theology/.

7. Strimple, "Amillennialism," 99.

8. Sam Storms, *Kingdom Come: The Amillennial Alternative* (n.p.: Christian Focus, 2016), 11.

9. Storms, *Kingdom Come*, 540–41.

10. Quoted in Kim Riddlebarger, *A Case for Amillennialism: Understanding the End Times* (Grand Rapids: Baker Books, 2013), 141, Kindle.

11. Riddlebarger, *Case for Amillennialism*, 146.

12. Riddlebarger, *Case for Amillennialism*, 151.

13. Riddlebarger, *Case for Amillennialism*, 154.

14. Anthony A. Hoekema, "Amillennialism," in *Meaning of the Millennium*, 156.

15. Hoekema, "Amillennialism," 156–57.

16. Strimple, "Amillennialism," 121–22.

17. Strimple, "Amillennialism," 123–24.

18. Douglas Kelly, "The Binding of Satan," Ligonier Ministries, November 25, 2013, https://www.ligonier.org/learn/articles/binding-satan.

19. Kelly, "Binding of Satan."

20. Strimple, "Amillennialism," 100.

21. Strimple, "Amillennialism," 120.

Chapter 9 Postmillennial View

1. Loraine Boettner, "Postmillennialism," in *Meaning of the Millennium*, 117.

2. J. Macleod, "Postmillennialism—Its Historical Development," Christian Study Library, accessed March 16, 2023, https://www.christianstudylibrary.org/article/post millennialism-%E2%80%93-its-historical-development.

3. Steven R. Pointer, "American Postmillennialism: Seeing the Glory," *Christian History* 61 (1999), https://www.christianitytoday.com/history/issues/issue-61/american -postmillennialism-seeing-glory.html.

4. Quoted in Kim Riddlebarger, "Princeton and the Millennium: A Study of American Postmillennialism," Grace Online Library, accessed March 16, 2023, https://graceon inelibrary.org/eschatology/postmillennialism/princeton-and-the-millennium-a-study -of-american-postmillennialism-by-kim-riddlebarger/.

5. Harvey Cox, "The Warring Visions of the Religious Right," *The Atlantic*, November 1995, 66, https://www.theatlantic.com/magazine/archive/1995/11/the-warring -visions-of-the-religious-right/376472/.

6. Quoted in Pointer, "American Postmillennialism."

7. Jack Jenkins, "As Christian Nationalism Digs In, Differing Visions Surface," Religion News Service, October 28, 2022, https://religionnews.com/2022/10/28/as-christian -nationalism-digs-in-will-differing-visions-clash/.

8. Jenkins, "Christian Nationalism Digs In."

9. See Riddlebarger, "Princeton and the Millennium."

10. Pointer, "American Postmillennialism."

11. Kenneth L. Gentry Jr., "Postmillennialism," in *Three Views*, 23–24.

12. Gentry, "Postmillennialism," 25.

13. Gentry, "Postmillennialism," 33–34.

14. Loraine Boettner, *The Millennium* (Phillipsburg, NJ: P&R, 1957), 36.

15. B. B. Warfield, "The Millennium and the Apocalypse," *The Princeton Theological Review* 2 (October 1904): 3.

16. Quoted in Gentry, "Postmillennialism," 50.

17. Gentry, "Postmillennialism," 50.

18. Gentry, "Postmillennialism," 51–52.

19. Boettner, "Postmillennialism," 126.

20. Boettner, "Postmillennialism," 126–32.

21. Clouse, "Introduction," 8.

22. Todd M. Johnson and Gina A. Zurlo, "Christian Martyrdom as a Pervasive Phenomenon," Gordon-Conwell Theological Seminary, https://www.gordonconwell .edu/wp-content/uploads/sites/13/2019/04/2Countingmartyrsmethodology.pdf.

23. For example, see this article from Mark Henry, one of those who argues for global progress: Mark Henry, "The Best Books on Global Progress," September 13, 2021, https://www.markhenry.ie/articles/the-best-books-on-global-progress.

24. Mike Aquilina and James L. Papandrea, *How Christianity Saved Civilization . . . and Must Do So Again* (Manchester, NH: Sophia Institute Press, 2019); Alvin J. Schmidt, *How Christianity Changed the World* (Grand Rapids: Zondervan, 2004); Jeremiah J. Johnston, *Unimaginable: What Our World Would Be Like without Christianity* (Bloomington, MN: Bethany House, 2017); Tom Holland, *Dominion: The Making of the Western Mind* (Boston: Little, Brown, 2019).

25. "Mind-Blowing Statistics about Christianity You Need to Know," *Holy Blog*, accessed March 16, 2023, https://www.holyart.com/blog/mind-blowing-statistics-christianity-need-know/.

Chapter 10 Which View Should I Believe?

1. Dr. Seuss, *Which Pet Should I Get?* (New York: Random House, 2015).

2. Ligonier Ministries, "Interpreting the Bible Literally," Ligonier.org, February 20, 2017, https://www.ligonier.org/learn/devotionals/interpreting-bible-literally.

3. *ESV Gospel Transformation Study Bible* (Wheaton: Crossway, 2019).

4. Howard G. Hendricks and William D. Hendricks, *Living By the Book: The Art and Science of Reading the Bible* (Chicago: Moody, 2007).

5. Gordon D. Fee and Douglas Stuart, *How to Read the Bible for All Its Worth*, 4th ed. (Grand Rapids: Zondervan, 2014).

6. Hamilton, *Basis of Millennial Faith*, 38.

7. Payne, *Encyclopedia of Biblical Prophecy*, 143.

8. Payne, *Encyclopedia of Biblical Prophecy*, 47.

9. Bernard Ramm, *Protestant Biblical Interpretation: A Textbook of Hermeneutics* (Grand Rapids: Baker, 1950), 172.

10. Tremper Longman III, *Daniel*, NIV Application Commentary (Grand Rapids: Zondervan, 1999), 226.

11. Joyce G. Baldwin, *Daniel: An Introduction and Commentary*, Tyndale Old Testament Commentaries (Downers Grove, IL: InterVarsity, 1978), 176.

12. Payne, *Encyclopedia of Biblical Prophecy*, 138–40.

13. Payne, *Encyclopedia of Biblical Prophecy*, 387–89.

14. Payne, *Encyclopedia of Biblical Prophecy*, 387–89.

15. Quoted in Thomas D. Ice, "What Is Replacement Theology?," Scholars Crossing, *Article Archives* 106 (2009), https://digitalcommons.liberty.edu/pretrib_arch/106/.

Chapter 11 The Hope All Christians Share, Part 1

1. Center for the Study of Global Christianity at Gordon-Conwell Theological Seminary, "How Do You Define a Denomination?," accessed May 26, 2023, https://www.gordonconwell.edu/center-for-global-christianity/research/quick-facts/.

2. Blomberg, *Case for Historic Premillennialism*, 118.

3. Stephen D. Morrison, "7 Theories of the Atonement Summarized," accessed March 16, 2023, https://www.sdmorrison.org/7-theories-of-the-atonement-summarized/.

4. Morrison, "7 Theories."

Chapter 12 The Hope All Christians Share, Part 2

1. Center for the Study of Global Christianity at Gordon-Conwell Theological Seminary, "Why Do You Report Such High Figures for Christian Martyrs?," accessed May 26, 2023, https://www.gordonconwell.edu/center-for-global-christianity/research /quick-facts/.

2. Emily McFarlan Miller, "Christian Persecution Higher than Ever as Open Doors' World Watch List Marks 30 Years," Religion News Service, January 17, 2023, https:// religionnews.com/2023/01/17/christian-persecution-higher-than-ever-as-open-doors -world-watch-list-marks-30-years/.

3. An important exception is Loraine Boettner in his book *The Millennium*, 67–75 and 405–8.

4. Quoted in Andy Woods, "Toward a New Ministry Paradigm, Part 2," Dispensational Publishing House blog, accessed March 16, 2023, https://dispensationalpublish ing.com/we-must-emphasize-prophecy-to-the-extent-that-scripture-emphasizes-it/.

5. David Hall, *The Millennium of Jesus Christ: An Exposition of the Revelation for All Ages* (Oak Ridge, TN: Covenant Foundation, 1998), 10–11.

6. Boettner, *The Millennium*, 410.

7. Nijay Gupta, "Reading Revelation through a Different Lens (Dean Flemming)," Patheos, October 3, 2022, https://www.patheos.com/blogs/cruxsola/2022/10/reading -revelation-through-a-different-lens-dean-flemming/.

8. Russell Moore, "Why I'm Losing My Millennium," *Christianity Today*, December 2021, 28.

9. John Piper, "What Does the New Testament Mean That Jesus Will Come Soon?," Crossway.org, January 24, 2023, https://www.crossway.org/articles/what-does-the-new -testament-mean-that-jesus-will-come-soon/.

10. C. S. Lewis, *The Last Battle* (New York: HarperCollins, 1956), 228.

11. C. S. Lewis, "The Weight of Glory," in *The Weight of Glory* (New York: Harper-Collins, 1949), 46.

12. C. S. Lewis, *The Problem of Pain* (New York: Macmillan, 1948), 115. See discussion in Bryan Chapell, *Unlimited Grace: The Heart Chemistry That Frees from Sin and Fuels the Christian Life* (Wheaton: Crossway, 2016), 169.

13. J. Oliver Buswell Jr., *A Systematic Theology of the Christian Religion*, 2 vols. (Grand Rapids: Zondervan, 1976), 2:315.

14. Boettner, *The Millennium*, 18.

Chapter 13 "Behold, I Am Making All Things New"

1. Helmut Thielicke, "But Man Fell on Earth," *Christianity Today*, March 4, 1977, https://www.christianitytoday.com/ct/1977/march-4/but-man-fell-on-earth.html.

2. Tim Keller, *Jesus the King: Understanding the Life and Death of the Son of God* (New York: Penguin, 2016), 55, 62.

3. Paul Tripp, "How to Never Lose Hope," PaulTripp.com, May 6, 2020, https:// www.paultripp.com/wednesdays-word/posts/how-to-never-lose-hope.

4. J.R.R. Tolkien, *The Lord of the Rings* (New York: Houghton Mifflin, 1954), 951–52.

Bryan Chapell, PhD, is president of Unlimited Grace Media, broadcasting daily grace-filled messages in most major US markets and streaming preaching instruction in 1,500 cities in over 90 nations. He also leads the administrative committee of the Presbyterian Church in America, is pastor emeritus of the historic Grace Presbyterian Church in Peoria, Illinois, and is president emeritus of Covenant Theological Seminary in St. Louis, Missouri. Dr. Chapell is an internationally renowned preacher, teacher, and speaker and the author of many books, including *Unlimited Grace, Each for the Other, Holiness by Grace, Promises of Grace, Praying Backwards, The Gospel according to Daniel, The Hardest Sermons You'll Ever Have to Preach, Christ-Centered Worship, Christ-Centered Sermons*, and *Christ-Centered Preaching*, a textbook now in multiple editions and many languages that has established him as one of this generation's foremost teachers of preaching. He and his wife, Kathy, have four adult children and a growing number of grandchildren.

CONNECT WITH BRYAN

bryanchapell.com

unlimitedgrace.com

www.oneplace.com/ministries/unlimited-grace